Springer Texts in Education

Springer Texts in Education delivers high-quality instructional content for graduates and advanced graduates in all areas of Education and Educational Research. The textbook series is comprised of self-contained books with a broad and comprehensive coverage that are suitable for class as well as for individual self-study. All texts are authored by established experts in their fields and offer a solid methodological background, accompanied by pedagogical materials to serve students such as practical examples, exercises, case studies etc. Textbooks published in the Springer Texts in Education series are addressed to graduate and advanced graduate students, but also to researchers as important resources for their education, knowledge and teaching. Please contact Yoka Janssen at Yoka.Janssen@springer.com or your regular editorial contact person for queries or to submit your book proposal.

Jill T. Tussey · Leslie Haas

Exploring Genre through Gamified Adventures in Elementary Classrooms

Jill T. Tussey
School of Education
Buena Vista University
Storm Lake, IA, USA

Leslie Haas
Division of Education and Counseling
Xavier University of Louisiana
New Orleans, LA, USA

This work contains media enhancements, which are displayed with a "play" icon. Material in the print book can be viewed on a mobile device by downloading the Springer Nature "More Media" app available in the major app stores. The media enhancements in the online version of the work can be accessed directly by authorized users.

ISSN 2366-7672   ISSN 2366-7680 (electronic)
Springer Texts in Education
ISBN 978-3-031-41716-0   ISBN 978-3-031-41717-7 (eBook)
https://doi.org/10.1007/978-3-031-41717-7

© The Editor(s) (if applicable) and The Author(s), under exclusive license to Springer Nature Switzerland AG 2023

This work is subject to copyright. All rights are solely and exclusively licensed by the Publisher, whether the whole or part of the material is concerned, specifically the rights of translation, reprinting, reuse of illustrations, recitation, broadcasting, reproduction on microfilms or in any other physical way, and transmission or information storage and retrieval, electronic adaptation, computer software, or by similar or dissimilar methodology now known or hereafter developed.

The use of general descriptive names, registered names, trademarks, service marks, etc. in this publication does not imply, even in the absence of a specific statement, that such names are exempt from the relevant protective laws and regulations and therefore free for general use.

The publisher, the authors, and the editors are safe to assume that the advice and information in this book are believed to be true and accurate at the date of publication. Neither the publisher nor the authors or the editors give a warranty, expressed or implied, with respect to the material contained herein or for any errors or omissions that may have been made. The publisher remains neutral with regard to jurisdictional claims in published maps and institutional affiliations.

This Springer imprint is published by the registered company Springer Nature Switzerland AG
The registered company address is: Gewerbestrasse 11, 6330 Cham, Switzerland

Paper in this product is recyclable.

Springer Nature More Media App

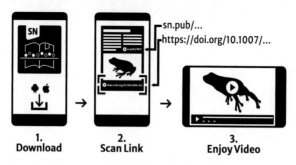

Support: customerservice@springernature.com

Contents

1 Kindergarten—Nursery Rhymes 1
  1.1 Quest Objectives 1
  1.2 Nursey Rhyme Four Quest Series Narrative Introduction 1
  1.3 Quest #1—Recall and Prewriting 3
  1.4 Quest #2—Speaking, Listening, and Resource Exploration 4
  1.5 Quest #3—Comprehension, Story Extension, and Problem
       Solving 8
  1.6 Quest #4—Art Integration 10
  1.7 Supplemental Resources 11

2 First Grade—Fairy Tales 15
  2.1 Quest Objectives 15
  2.2 Fairy Tale Four Quest Series Narrative Introduction 15
  2.3 Quest #1—Recall, Summarization, and Writing 17
  2.4 Quest #2—Speaking, Listening, and Resource Exploration 19
  2.5 Quest #3—Comprehension, Story Extension, and Problem
       Solving 23
  2.6 Quest #4—Art Integration 25
  2.7 Supplemental Resources 27

3 Second Grade—Fables 29
  3.1 Quest Objectives 29
  3.2 Fable Four Quest Series Narrative Introduction 31
  3.3 Quest #1—Storytelling and Presenting 31
  3.4 Quest #2—Speaking, Listening, and Resource Exploration 32
  3.5 Quest #3—Comprehensions, Story Extension, and Problem
       Solving 35
  3.6 Quest #4—Art Integration 37
  3.7 Supplemental Resources 38

4 Third Grade—Folktales 41
  4.1 Quest Objectives 41
  4.2 Four Quest Series Narrative Introduction 41
  4.3 Quest #1—Storytelling and Presenting 43

viii   Contents

4.4   Quest #2—Speaking, Listening, and Resource Exploration   44
4.5   Quest #3—Comprehension, Story Extension, and Problem
      Solving   48
4.6   Quest #4—Art Integration   50
4.7   Supplemental Resources   51

5   **Fourth Grade—Legends**   55
5.1   Quest Objectives   55
5.2   Legend Four Quest Series Narrative Introduction   57
5.3   Quest #1—Paraphrasing and Presenting   57
5.4   Quest #2—Speaking, Listening, and Resource Exploration   58
5.5   Quest #3—Comprehension, Story Extension, and Problem
      Solving   62
5.6   Quest #4—Art Intregration   63
5.7   Supplemental Resources   64

6   **Fifth Grade—Myths**   67
6.1   Quest Objectives   67
6.2   Four Quest Series Narrative Introduction   69
6.3   Quest #1—Storytelling and Presenting   69
6.4   Quest #2—Speaking, Listening, and Resource Exploration   70
6.5   Quest #3—Comprehension, Story Extension, and Problem
      Solving   74
6.6   Quest #4—Art Integration   75
6.7   Supplemental Resources   77

Getting Started

We are excited to share this book designed by and for elementary school teachers to support literacy practices in grades kindergarten through fifth grade! For the purposes of this book, we are using the definition of literacy available through the International Literacy Association (ILA) (n.d.) which explains this concept as "the ability to identify, understand, interpret, create, compute, and communicate using visual, audible, and digital materials across disciplines and in any context" (para. 14). Gamified learning experiences provided through narrative quests offer students literacy skill development across genres. This type of immersive engagement lends itself to skills development across disciplines (Bibi, 2021).

Chapter Components

Based on the ideas and structures embedded in quality games, this book incorporates disciplinary literacy through a series of quests within a fun and engaging environment. Games have historically provided players with targeted goals and opportunities for repeated practice. This can be seen through strategic problem solving in ancient, yet still relevant games like chess. Additionally, through trial and error, players develop skills and strategies to navigate through games to reach their objectives. Much like traditional games, this book provides students with opportunities to learn through targeted goals, repeated practice, and trial and error. Each chapter's objectives are based on bundled grade-level concepts, its rules provide structure for each lesson, and its outcomes are both formative and summative assessments. Furthermore, chapter objectives are based on national and international academic standards. Rules are provided via chapter-based questing systems, and outcomes can be observed through project development.

While each chapter features a different grade level and genre, the content follows a similar design across chapters. This organization begins with overarching literacy concepts that can easily be connected to state, national, and international standards. Next, students follow a series of magical adventures developed as narrative gameplay. Quest #1 focuses on reading and writing, Quest #2 focuses on listening, speaking, and resource exploration, Quest # 3 focuses on comprehension through project-based learning, and Quest #4 focuses on art integration. Chapters offer stand-alone experiences; however, resources to differentiate activities are available, allowing teachers to pull from more than one grade level or chapter. Therefore, each quest has the potential to provide opportunities for homogenous and heterogeneous student groupings within one grade level, between grade levels, or across schools. Resources and reproducible content are also available online to support students and teachers move through each quest.

Theoretical Framework

Multiple Literacies Theory (MLT) (Cope & Kalantzia, 2009; The New London Group, 1996) is founded on the idea that multiple modes of communication "differ based on culture and context and are constantly changing by and for users based on specific cultural purposes" (Haas & Tussey, 2021, p. 258). Additionally, it consists of four non-sequential constructs: situated practice, overt instruction, critical framing, and transformed practice. It also suggests that multiple literacies, like those embedded in gameplay, enlighten learners as "users, players, creators and discerning consumers rather than spectators, delegates, audiences or quiescent consumers" (Cope & Kalantzia, 2009, p. 172). According to Masny (2011), MLT provide that while literacy constitute texts, in a broad sense (for example, music, visual arts (painting, sculpting), physics, mathematics, digital remixes) that fuse with religion, gender, race, culture, and power, and that produce speakers, writers, artists, digital avatars: communities. Literacies are actualized according to a particular context in time and in space in which they operate (p. 339).

Therefore, MLT supports gameplay as literacy becomes about creation, exposure, reflection, and growth. MLT then becomes part of the framework which supports the development and use of gamified literacy as teaching and learning experiences.

Engagement Theory (ET) (Kearsley & Shneiderman,1998) is based on the idea that learning should be collaborative, project-based, and authentic. Furthermore, it supports the idea that technology has the ability to create unique ways of engaging learners. Kearsley and Shneiderman (1998) offer that "engagement theory is based upon the idea of creating successful collaborative teams that work on ambitious projects" (p. 20). The activities embedded in this book provide purposeful, project-based opportunities for engaged teaching and learning through gameplay in hands-on settings for real-world understandings. ET also reinforces the pedagogical practice of project-based learning (PBL), as PBL provides authentic, collaborative, and engaged learning opportunities to develop knowledge and skills through exploring and answering complex questions, problems, and/or challenges (Haas & Tussey, 2021; Miller, 2014). The Buck Institute for Education (BIE) PBL Works (n.d.) offers the idea that quality PBL should include student inquiry through authentic and challenging problems and/or questions, sustained inquiry, student voice and choice, reflection, critique, revision, and public product. Additionally, PBL pedagogical practices should facilitate classroom cultures through purposefully aligned and engaging lessons, managed activities, scaffolded understanding, and assessed learning. When PBL is embedded into teaching and learning, it can help "students develop 21st century skills including creativity, collaboration, and leadership and engages them in complex, real-world challenges that help them meet expectations for critical thinking" (USDE OET, 2017, p. 14).

Objectives

The seminal work of Marzano et al., (1997) related to the five dimensions of learning provided a considered framework while developing this book. These dimensions include (1) positive attitudes and perceptions about learning, (2) acquiring and integrating knowledge, (3) extending and refining knowledge, (4) using knowledge meaningfully, and (5) productive habits of mind. Incorporating the five dimensions throughout the planning and development process provided a structure on which to build student player experiences. Therefore, it is the aim of each embedded quest to offer students fun and engaging ways to interact, integrate, extend, and refine learning opportunities across disciplines utilizing critical, creative, and self-regulated thinking in meaningful ways. Each chapter's learning objectives are based on national and international standards and the knowledge and cognitive procedural dimensions of the revised Bloom's Taxonomy (Anderson et al., 2014). A grid is provided at the beginning of each chapter, adapted from the Iowa State University's Center for Excellence in Learning and Teaching (2020) model of learning objectives, and utilized to determine specific and measurable learning outcomes for each quest within each discipline. Literacy objective samples are provided. These objectives are tied to activities, assessments, lessons, and projects embedded in each chapter's questing system.

Quests

Quests are designed as a narrative roadmap to guide students through activities, projects, and resources. Additionally, quests provide a narrative, written in the chapter's featured genre, to guide students through objectives, rules, procedures, and clues. These narratives, along with many fiction offerings within the quests, can be enjoyed as read alouds, choral reading, or small group readings. According to ILA (n.d.), a read-aloud happens when someone, usually a teacher, orally reads a text and shares pictures, images, and/or words with a group of students. However, the purpose of a read-aloud "is to model proficient reading and language, promote conversation, motivate, and extend comprehension and conceptual understandings" (ILA, n.d., para. 2). Furthermore, reading aloud can provide listeners practice with foundational skills, opportunities with vocabulary, models of fluent reading, access to complex text, and opportunities to experience pleasure reading (Varlas, 2018). Going a step further and considering the classroom as a community of learners, Valas (2018) states, "read alouds can draw students of any age into a community that is knowledgeable and curious about topics and texts, from novels to news reports" (para. 1).

Teachers utilizing this book can differentiate through choices related to materials, time, and groupings. Additionally, teachers have the option of choosing different and/or additional resources other than those offered within the quests. Experience points, or XP, will be awarded at the end of each quest. Players will need to earn XP for each quest before advancing to the next in the series. Bonus XP can be earned throughout gameplay as individual students or groups of students make connections between activities, projects, and resources and can be awarded at the discretion of the teacher. Teachers may choose to tally XP earned from all four quests within the chapter as a summative assessment of the chapter's learning. XP can serve as a motivational tool as students work cooperatively to complete tasks.

Resources

Resources are embedded throughout the book. They include multimodal text sets developed specifically for each chapter. Text sets provide students and teachers with a variety of themed resources which offer opportunities for students to read both wide and deep on connected topics and offer support related to academic vocabulary, modality choice, schema development, and student engagement (Tussey, et al., 2020). A range of reading levels are also available for differentiation, individualization, and personalization. Copyright dates are varied, and multiple versions of stories are provided to give students opportunities to compare and contrast information across authors, locations, and time. Utilizing text sets to support learning activities can provide scaffolds for content area literacy learning, as well as support culturally and linguistically responsive teaching and learning. Teachers are highly encouraged to check out each text set available regardless of the grade you teach, as they offer high-quality multimodal resources.

In support of each chapter, many resources are available to help guide both teachers and students through each quest. These resources include reproducible student quests, student activity cards, and student XP cards. Online teacher project planning guides and online multimodal text sets are also available. The book's authors have worked as practicing kindergarten through fifth grade teachers and understand that cost can often be a deterrent for activities and projects like those associated with this book. With that in mind, the text sets provided are available either through open-source avenues or are available at local libraries. Project materials have been thoughtfully considered, and the majority can be procured through recycled or donated home goods such as aluminum foil, plastic bowls, and playing cards and/or are common classroom materials and supplies.

As a practicing teacher, time is limited and valued. Teachers need instructional support that will help make the most out of the little time they have. That's why being able to bundle standards to teach multiple concepts within one easy to implement lesson activity is essential. This book offers many types of bundled, effective, and engaging activities while also taking the work out of finding resources. The intent of this book is to help you work smarter, rather than harder, and we hope you enjoy implementing these activities as much as we enjoyed creating them. Happy Teaching!

References

Anderson, L., Krathwohl, D., & Bloom, B. (2014). *A taxonomy for learning, teaching, and assessing: A revision of Bloom's taxonomy of educational objectives.* Pearson.

Bibi, N. (2021). Effect of activity-based games on students' academic achievement in social sciences. *FWU Journal of Social Sciences, 15*(3), 82–95. https://doi.org/10.51709/19951272/Fall-2021/5.

Cope, B., & Kalantzis, M. (2009). "Multiliteracies": New literacies, new learning. *Pedagogies, 4*(3), 164–195.

Haas, L., & Tussey, J. (2021). Equity and engagement through digital storytelling and game-based learning. In L. Haas, & J. Tussey (Eds.), *Connecting disciplinary literacy to digital storytelling in K-12 education* (pp. 257–277). IGI Global.

International Literacy Association. (n.d.). *Literacy glossary.* Retrieved from https://www.literacyworldwide.org/get-resources/literacy-glossary

Iowa State University Center for Excellence in Learning and Teaching. (2020). *Revised Bloom's taxonomy.* https://www.celt.iastate.edu/teaching/effective-teaching-practices/revised-blooms taxonomy/

Kearsley, G., & Shneiderman, B. (1998). Engagement theory: A framework for technology-based teaching and learning. *Educational Technology, 38*(5), 20–23.

Marzano, R. J., Pickering, D. J., Arredondo, D. E. (1997). In association for supervision and curriculum development, & mid-continent regional educational laboratory. *Dimensions of learning: Teacher's manual.* Association for Supervision and Curriculum Development.

Masny, D. (2011). Multiple literacies theory: How it functions, what it produces. *Prospectiva, 28,* 337–352.

Miller, A. (2014). How can project-based learning motivate students even further? *ASCE InServe.* https://inservice.ascd.org/how-can-project-based-learning-motivate-students-even-further/

Neuman, S. (2015). Explaining and understanding early literacy. *Investigaciones Sobre Lectura,* 7–14. https://doi.org/10.37132/isl.v0i2.1

The New London Group. (1996, Spring). A pedagogy of multiliteracies: Designing social futures. *Harvard Educational Review, 66,* 1. http://newarcproject.pbworks.com/f/Pedagogy+of+Multil iteracies_New+London+Group.pdf

Tussey, J., Haas, L., & Garling, B. (2020). Bye-bye basal: Multimodal texts in the classroom. In P. M. Sullivan, J. L. Lantz, & B. A. Sullivan (Eds.), *Handbook of research on integrating digital technology with literacy pedagogies* (pp. 192–211). IGI Global.

United States Department of Education's Office of Educational Technology. (2010). *Transforming American education: Learning powered by technology.* https://www.ed.gov/sites/default/files/NETP-2010-final-report.pdf

Varlas, L. (2018). *Why every class needs read alouds. ASCD Education Update, 60*(1). http://www.ascd.org/publications/newsletters/education-update/jan18/vol60/num01/Why-Every-Class-Needs-Read-Alouds.aspx

About the Authors

Dr. Jill T. Tussey's career in literacy education has provided a variety of experiences in curriculum and instruction across K-12, undergraduate, and graduate courses. Her areas of interest include student engagement and motivation with targeted focus on digital literacy, poverty impacts, and social-emotional learning. Service leadership is important to Dr. Tussey and can be clearly seen in her current work as Division Chair for Literacy, TESL, and Early Childhood at Buena Vista University. She has authored and edited books, chapters, and journal articles. Additionally, she has presented at local, state, national, and international settings over a variety of literacy topics.

Dr. Leslie Haas Teaching experiences across her career include working with K-12, undergraduate, and graduate students. Additional experiences include instructional coaching, professional development, curriculum design, and department administration. Opportunities in highly diverse settings have acted as both a catalyst and a foundation for her focus on integrating and connecting literacy across disciplines through culturally and linguistically responsive instructional practices. Dr. Haas is particularly interested in technology-based literacy opportunities for underrepresented populations through engagement with popular culture, specifically gaming and fanfiction. She has been honored for her work in research, teaching, and technology through Buena Vista University, Fierce Education, The Texas A&M University System, and The Dallas Catholic Foundation.

Kindergarten—Nursery Rhymes

1

Kindergarten academic experiences should be engaging and fun! This chapter offers playful adventures situated in the world of nursery rhymes. Adventures are embedded with targeted learning objectives and incorporate multiple activities, readings, resources, and projects. Additionally, chapter resources can be shared with families as a support for the exploration and development of academic, social, and emotional concepts.

1.1 Quest Objectives

Learning objectives focused on kindergarten literacy are based on national and international standards and are provided in a grid format. Objectives explored within the questing systems, can be used as a foundation for future lessons, and/or may be utilized as a review for past learning. A comprehensive overview of the development of quest objectives can be found in the "Getting Started" section of the book. Overarching learning objectives are provided at the beginning of each quest.

To read the grid, look at where the knowledge dimension and cognitive procedural dimension meet (Table 1.1).

1.2 Nursey Rhyme Four Quest Series Narrative Introduction

Quest #1 focuses on the developing a foundation of understanding through anchor texts, Quest #2 highlights text set resources and the development of speaking and listening skills, Quest #3 targets comprehension through project-based learning,

© The Author(s), under exclusive license to Springer Nature Switzerland AG 2023
J. T. Tussey and L. Haas, *Exploring Genre through Gamified Adventures in Elementary Classrooms*, Springer Texts in Education, https://doi.org/10.1007/978-3-031-41717-7_1

Table 1.1 Learning objective examples for kindergarten literacy

	Knowledge Dimension	Knowledge Dimension	Knowledge Dimension	Knowledge Dimension
	Factual	Conceptual	Procedural	Metacognitive
Cognitive Procedural Dimension Remember	Students will be able to list key events	Students will be able to recognize story elements and visuals when shared by their peers	Students will be able to recall important events in the nursery rhymes	Students will be able to identify which images support the retelling of the nursery rhyme
Cognitive Procedural Dimension Understand	Students will be able to summarize their understanding	Students will be able to classify important components to be included in gameplay over nursery rhymes	Students will be able to clarify elements of the nursery rhymes with visuals	Students will be able to make predictions about what tools will be needed to build the products
Cognitive Procedural Dimension Apply	Students will be able to respond to questions asked by adults and peers	Students will be able to provide their understanding of the nursery rhymes to their peers	Students will be able to carry out project-based tasks	Students will be able to use a variety of resources and tools
Cognitive Procedural Dimension Analyze	Students will be able to select visuals that support their understanding	Students will be able to differentiate between main events in the nursery rhymes	Students will be able to integrate background knowledge to build products to support the main characters	Students will be able to deconstruct the process needed to create the tools to support the main characters
Cognitive Procedural Dimension Evaluate	Students will be able to check multiple resources to complete tasks	Students will be able to determine which resources to utilize to complete quests	Students will be able to judge the important information from each resource	Students will be able to reflect over content from multiple resources

(continued)

1.3 Quest #1—Recall and Prewriting

Table 1.1 (continued)

	Knowledge Dimension	Knowledge Dimension	Knowledge Dimension	Knowledge Dimension
	Factual	Conceptual	Procedural	Metacognitive
Cognitive Procedural Dimension Create	Students will be able to generate ideas and questions based on the nursery rhymes	Students will be able to assemble tools and resources to complete projects tied to the nursery rhymes	Students will be able to design tools to help the characters in the nursery rhymes	Students will be able to create products connected to each main character

Concrete ——> Abstract

and Quest #4 centers on a multimodal art integration. The nursery rhymes featured throughout the four quest series are the Humpty Dumpty, Itsy Bitsy Spider, and Jack and Jill. An overview of how quests are developed are available in the "Getting Started" section of this book. Additional quest support can be found in the supplemental resource section of this chapter.

> **Nursey Rhyme Quest Narrative Introduction**
> Fran and Stan went to the shelf.
>
> To choose the silliest book.
>
> Fran found one and then was done,
>
> While Stan continued to look.

1.3 Quest #1—Recall and Prewriting

Below, Kindergarten Quest #1 is presented in a grid format. It was designed to develop student schema through anchor texts as well as support student writing. Differentiated pedagogical strategies are listed in *Kindergarten Quest #1 Additional Teacher Information* section of the grid provided below.

Kindergarten Quest #1 *Nursery Rhymes and Choice!*
Kindergarten Quest #1 Focus Nursery Rhymes and Writing
Kindergarten Quest #1 Overarching Objective Develop recall and prewriting skills

(continued)

(continued)

Kindergarten Quest #1 Description Fran and Stan loved nursery rhymes And liked to play pretend Stan liked to dance, and Fran liked to prance, And they never wanted it to end One day in the park they heard a silly little rhyme, And decided to take a look Fran saw a spout and Stan started to shout, When water ran down a book The book was showing a story About a spider and the sun Stan thought it was strange and Fran stayed out of range, But the spider seemed to have fun The spider smiled at the kids And handed them a screen Fran took hold and Stan was bold As he began to watch the scene https://www.youtube.com/watch?v=w_lCi8U49mY
Kindergarten Quest #1 Assessment and Completion When the video is over, the teacher will explain that this nursery rhyme begins the first quest in a set of adventures. Students will complete this first quest of four and be granted access to the next in the series. In order to complete the first quest, students must take turns retelling the story to one another. Next, have them draw events from the story and encourage students to label their drawings and/or act as a scribe and label them with students. Last, they will share *Itsy Bitsy Spider* and their drawing with others. Once all three activities are complete, students will earn five XP and gain access to the next quest. Reproducible XP cards are available at the end of this chapter and online
Kindergarten Quest #1 Additional Teacher Information The video students are asked to watch can be found at https://www.youtube.com/watch?v=w_l Ci8U49mY or at http://www.lesliehaasandjilltussey.com/teacher-resources.html. Watching the video can be facilitated either as a whole-group or in small-groups. Teachers may differentiate the summarizing task through student groupings, utilizing closed captioning, and periodic checks for understanding. During the sharing portion of this activity, it is recommended that students from other classes or grade levels become audience members. Awarding extra XP is encouraged for work exhibiting notable qualities. Examples include, but are not limited to: support of others and time on task

1.4 Quest #2—Speaking, Listening, and Resource Exploration

Below you will find Kindergarten Quest #2. This quest is designed for students to work in partners. Each partner will choose a resource treasure box. Individual students will be responsible for reviewing their treasure box and choosing resources to share with their partner. Next, students will play Simon Says in the same way Fran and Stan do so within the quest narrative. Differentiated pedagogical strategies are listed in *Kindergarten #2 Additional Teacher Information* section of the grid provided below.

1.4 Quest #2—Speaking, Listening, and Resource Exploration

Kindergarten Quest #2
Treasure Box Discovery

Kindergarten Quest #2 Focus
Speaking and Listening

Kindergarten Quest #2 Overarching Objective
Develop speaking and listening skills through gameplay and supported by multiple resources

Kindergarten Quest #2 Description
Fran and Stan wanted more books
After the rhyme was done
Stan looked down, and Fran looked around
But they couldn't find one
At the same time they noticed a large box
And felt much delight
Fran looked inside, and Stan suddenly cried
Because they couldn't believe their sight
The box was full of much treasure
And they couldn't believe their eyes
Stan reached in, and Fran felt a grin
From discovering such a prize
The treasure box began to speak
And tell the kids what to do
Fran got still, and Stan felt a chill
As the box spoke to the two
Simon Says is a game we will play
If you want to explore
Stan said, "I guess", and Fran said, "yes."
And the box began with more
The game about listening was explained
And the kids began to play
Fran was all ears, and Stan began to hear
How to listen and obey
Once the children won the game,
They earned a special prize
Stan felt smart, and Fran loved the art
Found with this box of supplies

Kindergarten Quest #2 Assessment and Completion
After reading the quest narrative, the teacher will explain that Simon Says is a game about listening and speaking. The children must pay careful attention in order to win the game. It is recommended that the teacher act as Simon the first several times the game is played. Once students clearly understand the rules, the teacher can give students an opportunity to act as Simon after playing several rounds of the game. The game may be repeated as many times as the teacher likes. Students can earn 15 XP for clearly speaking and carefully listening throughout the game

Kindergarten Quest #2 Additional Teacher Information
Resources for this quest can be found in the section titled *Books: Treasure Box of Nursery Rhymes* and *Digital Discoveries: Treasure Box of Nursery Rhymes* within this chapter and at http://www.lesliehaasandjilltussey.com/teacher-resources.html. Teachers may differentiate this task through student groupings based on academic literacy level, native language, and/or social-emotional maturity. Awarding extra XP may be offered for engagement, kindness, and sportsmanship

Books: treasure box of nursery rhymes

Fiction
- Kelly, M. (2017). *Big book of nursery rhymes.* Miles Kelly
- Parragon Books. (2018). *Mother goose treasury: A beautiful collection of favorite nursery rhymes.* Parragon Books

Humpty Dumpty
- Corn, J. (2015). *If Humpty Dumpty didn't fall: A new look at a classic nursery rhyme.* CreateSpace Independent Publishing Platform
- Horowitz, D. (2011). *Humpty Dumpty climbs again.* Puffin Books
- Kirk, D. (2000). *Humpty Dumpty.* Putnam Juvenile
- Levinthal, D. (2012). *Who pushed Humpty Dumpty?: and other notorious nursery tale mysteries.* Schwartz & Wade
- Pagnoni, R. (2010). *Humpty Dumpty's nursery rhymes.* B.E.S
- Pye, K. (2020). *Breaking News!: A story about Humpty Dumpty and change.* HeadStart Thinking
- Ranso, J. (2010). *What really happened to Humpty?* Charlesbridge
- Santat, D. (2017). *After the fall (how Humpty Dumpty got back up again).* Roaring Brook Press
- Stewart, J. & Salem, L. (2000). *Humpty Dumpty.* Continental Press

Eggs
- Coxe, M. (1997). *Big egg.* Random House Books for Young Readers
- John, J. (2019). *The good egg.* HarperCollins
- Seuss, D. (1960). *Green eggs and ham.* Beginner Books/Random House
- Seuss, D. (2004). *Horton hatches the egg.* Random House Books for Young Readers
- Seuss, D. (1953). *Scrambled eggs super!* Random House Books for Young Readers
- Stevens, J. & Crummel, S. (2019). *The donkey egg.* HMH Books for Young Readers

Jack and Jill
- Collins, H. (2003). *Jack and Jill.* Kids Can Press
- Pierce, T. (2018). *Jack and Jill and t-ball Bill.* Random House for Young Readers
- Salem, L. & Stewart, J. (2002). *Jack and Jill.* Continental Press
- Weston, M. (2002). *Jack and Jill and big dog Bill.* Random House for Young Readers
- Woodruff, L. (2010). *Jack and Jill.* Childs World Inc

Itsy Bitsy Spider
- Burton, J. (2016). *The itsy bitsy pilgrim.* Little Simon
- Burton, J. (2016). *The itsy bitsy reindeer.* Little Simon
- Burton, J. (2015). *The itsy bitsy snowman.* Little Simon
- Chapman, K. (2006). *Itsy bitsy spider.* Tiger Tales
- Emberley, R. (2013). *The itsy bitsy spider.* Two Little Birds
- Fry, S. (2014). *The itsy bitsy pumpkin.* Little Simon
- Dean, J. & Dean, K. (2019). *Pete the cat and the itsy bitsy spider.* HarperCollins
- Trapani, I. (1998). *The itsy bitsy spider.* Charlesbridge

Spiders
- Barton, B. (2019). *I'm trying to love spiders.* Puffin Books
- Burke, S.D. (2020). *Spider...the celebrity.* DoodleFace Publishing
- Carle, E. (1995). *The very busy spider.* World of Eric Carle

(continued)

(continued)

Books: treasure box of nursery rhymes

Non-fiction
Humpty Dumpty
Eggs
- Aston, D. (2014). *An egg is quiet.* Chronicle Books
- Jenkins, M. (2002). *The emperor's egg: Read and wonder.* Candlewick
- Jenkins, P. (2015). *A nest full of eggs.* HarperCollins
- Hauber, M. (2014). *The book of eggs: A life-size guide to the eggs of six hundred of the world's bird species.* University of Chicago Press
Jack and Jill
Water
- Portis, A. (2019). *Hey, water!* Neal Porter Books
- Stewart, M. (2014). *National geographic readers: Water.* National Geographic Kids
Itsy Bitsy Spider
Spiders
- Bedoyere, C. (2019). *100 facts: Spiders.* Miles Kelly
- Editors of TIME for Kids. (2005). *Time for Kids: Spiders!* HarperCollins
- Gibbons, G. (1993). *Spiders.* Holiday House
- Johnston, S. (2020). *Insects for kids: A junior scientist's guide to bees, butterflies, and other flying insects.* Rockridge Press
- Marsh, L. (2011). *National geographic readers: Spiders.* National Geographic Kids
- Silva, K. (2015). *Spiders: Amazing pictures & fun facts on animals in nature.* CreateSpace Independent Publishing Platform

Digital Discoveries: treasure box of nursery rhymes

Articles/Websites
- Little Learning Corner. (2020). *15 best nursery rhymes for kids.* Retrieved November 6, 2020 from https://littlelearningcorner.com/2019/05/nursery-rhymes-for-kids.html
Humpty Dumpty
- Mother Goose. (2020). *Humpty Dumpty sat on a wall.* Poetry Foundation. https://www.poetry foundation.org/poems/46951/humpty-dumpty-sat-on-a-wall
- The Editors. (2020). *How to collect and clean chicken eggs.* The Old Farmer's Almanac. https://www.almanac.com/raising-chickens-101-collecting-storing-and-hatching-chicken-eggs
Jack and Jill
- All Nursery Rhymes. (2020). *Jack and Jill.* Retrieved November 29, 2020 from https://allnur seryrhymes.com/jack-and-jill/
- Britannica Kids. (2020). *Water.* Retrieved November 29, 2020 from https://kids.britannica. com/kids/article/water/390625
- Climate Kids. (2020). *10 interesting things about water.* Nasa. https://climatekids.nasa.gov/ 10-things-water/
Itsy Bitsy Spider
- All Nursery Rhymes. (2020). *Itsy bitsy spider.* Retrieved November 29, 2020 from https://all nurseryrhymes.com/itsy-bitsy-spider/
- San Diego Kids. (2020). *Spider.* Retrieved November 29, 2020 from https://kids.sandiegozoo. org/animals/spider
- Science Kids. (2020). *Fun spider facts for kids.* Retrieved November 29, 2020 from https:// www.sciencekids.co.nz/sciencefacts/animals/spider.html

(continued)

(continued)

Digital Discoveries: treasure box of nursery rhymes
Movies/Videos *Humpty Dumpty* • Cockatiel Companion and the Pheasantasiam. (2013). *Bird egg size comparison.* YouTube. https://www.youtube.com/watch?v=-ecUnzv-1u4 • Science at Sheffield. (2018). *Why are bird eggs different shapes?* YouTube. https://www.youtube.com/watch?v=e-189LIYa0Y • Super Simple Songs—Kids Songs. (2017). *Humpty Dumpty.* YouTube. https://www.youtube.com/watch?v=nrv495corBc *Jack and Jill* • Geethanjali Kids. (2015). *Jack and jill nursery rhyme with lyrics.* YouTube. https://www.youtube.com/watch?v=XutKJalbixY • Periwinkle. (2019). *Importance of water: Science for kids.* YouTube. https://www.youtube.com/watch?v=c-3KCzxEgek *Itsy Bitsy Spider* • Happy Learning English. (2017). *Interesting facts about spiders.* YouTube. https://www.youtube.com/watch?v=CTCJwemsQEA • Homeschool Pop. (2018). *Spiders for kids.* YouTube. https://www.youtube.com/watch?v=IRZcbeCSoYQ • Little Angel: Nursery Rhymes & Kids Songs. (2016). *Itsy bitsy spider nursery rhyme: Kids songs.* YouTube. https://www.youtube.com/watch?v=TRcDPd3VY0M

1.5 Quest #3—Comprehension, Story Extension, and Problem Solving

Below you will find three options for *Kindergarten Quest #3*. These quests are designed for students to explore concepts through project-based learning. Each option will be divided into two sections. One section will contain the objective and description to be read before beginning the project. The second section, containing the completion and assessment, is to be read after the project is finished. Differentiated pedagogical strategies are listed in *Kindergarten Quest #3 Additional Teacher Information* section of all three quests in the grids provided below.

Option I—Kindergarten Quest #3 *Save Yourself!*	Option II—Kindergarten Quest #3 *Sticky Business!*	Option III—Kindergarten Quest #3 *Water Travel!*
Kindergarten Quest #3 Focus Comprehension, Story Extension, and Problem-Solving		

(continued)

1.5 Quest #3—Comprehension, Story Extension, and Problem Solving

(continued)

Option I—Kindergarten Quest #3 *Save Yourself!*	Option II—Kindergarten Quest #3 *Sticky Business!*	Option III—Kindergarten Quest #3 *Water Travel!*
Option I—Kindergarten Quest #3 Overarching Objective Utilize gained knowledge and engage in cooperative, project-based learning and problem solving to develop a tool that Humpty Dumpty could use to save himself	**Option II—Kindergarten Quest #3 Overarching Objective** Utilize gained knowledge and engage in cooperative, project-based learning and problem solving to create a spiderweb and see how many things it can hold	**Option III—Kindergarten Quest #3 Overarching Objective** Utilize gained knowledge and engage in cooperative, project-based learning and problem solving to design an alternate way for Jack to carry water down the hill
Option I—Kindergarten Quest #3 Description Fran and Stan had a great time Simon Says was fun Stan felt jolly and Fran liked folly, But they were sad to be done Stan and Fran wanted a new game They didn't want to wait Fran liked to discover and Stan liked to uncover They were ready to create Fran and Stan had a new task It was time to make a tool Stan liked sticks, and Fran liked bricks; They considered making a stool	**Option II—Kindergarten Quest #3 Description** Fran and Stan had a great time Simon Says was fun Stan felt jolly and Fran liked folly, But they were sad to be done Stan and Fran wanted a new game They didn't want to wait Fran liked to discover and Stan liked to uncover They were ready to create Fran and Stand had a new task To create a spider home Stan liked sticky and Fran thought it tricky; So they considered using foam	**Option III—Kindergarten Quest #3 Description** Fran and Stan had a great time Simon Says was fun Stan felt jolly and Fran liked folly, But they were sad to be done Stan and Fran wanted a new game They didn't want to wait Fran liked to discover and Stan liked to uncover They were ready to create Fran and Stan had a new task It was time to design a device Stan liked cars and Fran liked jars; So they tried using both

Kindergarten Quest #3 Assessment and Completion
Students will create projects through trial and error and through the use of a variety of materials. They will then share their creations with classmates to earn 20 XP and have access to the next adventure

Kindergarten Quest #3 Additional Teacher Information
Teachers may differentiate these tasks through student groupings or time on task. Additionally, material choice can be differentiated based on teacher and student choice. It is recommended that students be allowed to present their projects to other classes of children. For Option I, consider offering materials such as popsicle sticks or clay that would allow students to create a tool for Humpty Dumpty to get off the wall. For Option II, consider using glue and string and/or paste and yarn to develop spider webs. For Option III, consider using play dough to create a variety of vessels that can hold water. Awarding extra XP is encouraged for collaboration, cooperation, and creativity

1.6 Quest #4—Art Integration

Below you will find Kindergarten Quest #4. These quests are designed for students to explore literacy concepts through art. Each option will be divided into two sections. One section will contain the objective and description to be read before beginning the project. The second section, containing the completion and assessment, is to be read after the project is finished. Differentiated pedagogical strategies are listed in *Kindergarten Quest #4 Additional Teacher Information* section of all three quests in the grids provided below.

Option I—Kindergarten Quest #4 *Time to Decorate!*	Option II—Kindergarten Quest #4 *Looking Good!*	Option III—Kindergarten Quest #4 *Two Kinds of Crown*
Kindergarten Quest #4 Focus Literacy development through art exploration		
Option I—Kindergarten Quest #4 Overarching Objective Engage in critical thinking to consider how the setting enhances the story by having students redecorate Humpty Dumpty's wall	**Option II—Kindergarten Quest #4 Overarching Objective** Engage in critical thinking to consider how physical appearance might influence character feelings by giving the Itsy Bitsy Spider a makeover	**Option III—Kindergarten Quest #4 Overarching Objective** Engage in critical thinking to consider how appearance might portray personality by having students either create bandages Jack's head or create an actual crown
Option I—Kindergarten Quest #4 Description Fran and Stan enjoyed making stuff They really liked to design Stan wanted more, and Fran loved to explore It was their time to shine Stan and Fran had a new project This time it was making art Fran like to use glue, and Stan wasn't sure what to do But they knew they were smart Fran and Stan helped the wall shine They wanted it to glow Stan used string, and Fran drew wings Their wall was now ready to show	**Option II—Kindergarten Quest #4 Description** Fran and Stan enjoyed making stuff They really liked to design Stan wanted more, and Fran loved to explore It was their time to shine Stan and Fran had a new project This time it was making art Fran like to use glue, and Stan wasn't sure what to do But they knew they were smart Fran and Stan helped the spider shine They wanted her to glow Stan used lotion, and Fran sprayed potion Now the spider was ready to go	**Option III—Kindergarten Quest #4 Description** Fran and Stan enjoyed making stuff They really liked to design Stan wanted more, and Fran loved to explore It was their time to shine Stan and Fran had a new project This time it was making art Fran like to use glue, and Stan wasn't sure what to do But they knew they were smart Fran and Stan heard Jack whine He was covered in dirt Stan saw red, and Fran felt dread They wanted to help him with this hurt
Kindergarten Quest #4 Assessment and Completion Students will share their art projects with others and earn 25 XP. As this is the final quest, encourage students to continue thinking creatively while listening to stories, telling stories, watching stories, and eventually reading stories		

(continued)

(continued)

Option I—Kindergarten Quest #4 *Time to Decorate!*	Option II—Kindergarten Quest #4 *Looking Good!*	Option III—Kindergarten Quest #4 *Two Kinds of Crown*

Kindergarten Quest #4 Additional Teacher Information
Teachers may differentiate these tasks through student groupings or time on task. Additionally, material choice can be differentiated based on teacher and student choice. It is recommended that this art be displayed on a bulletin board either in the classroom or hallway. For Option I, consider sharing and discussing images related to story settings. For Option II, consider discussing how appearance might impact feelings and show images of animals and people that seem happy versus those that appear mad. For Option III, consider discussing the different meanings of the word "crown" and providing images to support these different definitions. Awarding extra XP is encouraged for collaboration, cooperation, and creativity

1.7   Supplemental Resources

Supplemental resources available in this section can also be found on https://sn.pub/Kjg4qA. These include:

- Reproducible XP score cards
- Additional teacher resources

Treasure Boxes for Books and Digital Discoveries can also be found on https://sn.pub/Kjg4qA.

Kindergarten Player Name(s)			
Quest #1	Quest #1 XP Earned	Quest #1 Extra XP Earned	Quest #1 Overall XP
Quest #2	Quest #2 XP Earned	Quest #2 Extra XP Earned	Quest #2 Overall XP
Quest #3	Quest #3 XP Earned	Quest #3 Extra XP Earned	Quest #3 Overall XP
Quest #4	Quest #4 XP Earned	Quest #4 Extra XP Earned	Quest #4 Overall XP
	Quest XP Total	Extra XP Total	Overall XP Total

Kindergarten Player Name(s)			
Quest #1	Quest #1 XP Earned	Quest #1 Extra XP Earned	Quest #1 Overall XP

(continued)

(continued)

Kindergarten Player Name(s)			
Quest #2	Quest #2 XP Earned	Quest #2 Extra XP Earned	Quest #2 Overall XP
Quest #3	Quest #3 XP Earned	Quest #3 Extra XP Earned	Quest #3 Overall XP
Quest #4	Quest #4 XP Earned	Quest #4 Extra XP Earned	Quest #4 Overall XP
	Quest XP Total	Extra XP Total	Overall XP Total

Additional Teacher Resources

Speaking and Listening Activities

- Students will dress up as a favorite character and share information about them
- Students will perform their favorite nursery rhyme
- Students will select two nursery rhymes and share how they are the same and how they are different
- Students will go on a scavenger hunt to find items in a selected nursery rhymes

Art Activities

- *Humpty Dumpty*: Humpty Dumpty needs his wall redecorated! Design a new wall
- *Jack and Jill*: Jack broke his crown! Create a new crown for him
- *Itsy Bitsy Spider*: Itsy Bitsy needs a make-over! Create your own Itsy Bitsy Spider

Additional Nursery Rhyme Treasure Boxes

1.7 Supplemental Resources

Books: treasure box of nursery rhymes

Fiction

Hey Diddle Diddle
- Bunting, E. (2011). *Hey diddle diddle.* Boyds Mills Press
- Crow, N. (2017). *Hey diddle diddle: Sign along with me!* Nosy Crow
- dePaola, T. (1998). *Hey diddle diddle & other mother goose rhymes.* Puffin Books
- Pixton, A. (2010). *Indestructibles: Hey diddle diddle.* Workman Publishing Company
- Stevens, J. (2001). *And the dish ran away with the spoon.* HMH Books for Young Readers

Animals
- Cummings, T. (2018). *Can I be your dog?* Random House Books for Young Readers
- Jr. Martin, B. (2013). *Kitty cat, kitty cat, are you waking up?* Two Lions
- Lemon, P. (2018). *The fed-up cow.* Quirky Picture Press
- Numeroff, L. (2008). *If you give a cat a cupcake.* Harper Collins
- Numeroff, L. (2011). *If you give a dog a donut.* Harper Collins
- Rabe, T. (2013). *What cat is that?: All about cats.* Random House Books for Young Readers
- Tingen, P. (2015). *A cat named mouse.* Patti Tingen
- Worth, B. (2018). *Cows can moo! Can you?* Random House Books for Younger Readers
- Zion, G. (2006). *Harry the dirty dog.* HarperCollins

Non-fiction

Hey Diddle Diddle
- Kapchinske, P. (2011). *Hey diddle diddle: A food chain tale.* Sylvan Dell Publishing

Animals
- Aliki. (1992). *Milk: From cow to carton.* HarperCollins
- Baines, B. (2012). *National geographic kids everything dogs: All the canine facts, photos, and fun you can get your paws on!* National Geographic Kids
- Carney, E. (2017). *National geographic readers: Woof! 100 fun facts about dogs.* National Geographic Kids
- Crisp, M. (2003). *Everything cat: What kids really want to know about cats.* Cooper Square Publishing LLC
- Davidson, J. (2014). *Cows for kids.* CreateSpace Independent Publishing Platform
- DK. (2018). *The everything book of cats and kittens.* DK Children
- Gagne, T. (2017). *The dog encyclopedia for kids.* Capstone Young Readers
- Lee, C. (2020). *Facts on cows.* Independently published
- Meister, C. (2016). *Cows.* Jump!
- Michaelson, C. (2020). *The wonderful book of kittens.* Independently published
- Michaelson, C. (2020). *The wonderful book of puppies.* Independently published
- Scott, T. (2018). *Radiant: Farm animals up close and personal.* Princeton Architectural Press
- Smalls, J. (2020). *This cat loves that!: A cat book for kids.* Rockridge Press
- Strattin, L. (2019). *Facts about cows.* Independently published

Digital discoveries: treasure box of nursery rhymes

Articles/Websites
- Little Learning Corner. (2020). *15 best nursery rhymes for kids.* Retrieved November 6, 2020 from https://littlelearningcorner.com/2019/05/nursery-rhymes-for-kids.html

Hey Diddle Diddle
- American Kennel Club. (2020). *Dog breeds.* Retrieved November 23, 2020 from https://www.akc.org/dog-breeds/
- Carolynkaye. (2020). *Cat care 101: A guide for new cat owners.* PetHelpful. https://pethelpful.com/cats/cat-care-101
- Mother Goose. (2020). *Hey, diddle, diddle.* Poetry Foundation. https://www.poetryfoundation.org/poems/46952/hey-diddle-diddle

Movies/Videos
Hey Diddle Diddle
- BBC Earth. (2019). *The best dogs of the BBC Earth.* YouTube. https://www.youtube.com/watch?v=MPV2METPeJU
- ErinsAnimals. (2015). *The history of housecats.* YouTube. https://www.youtube.com/watch?v=De-WJ5RDqXg
- Kelly's Animal Hospital. (2020). *How to take care of a puppy.* YouTube. https://www.kellysanimalhospital.com/services/dogs/puppy-care
- Little Baby Bum—Nursery Rhymes & Kids Songs. (2014). *Hey diddle diddle.* YouTube. https://www.youtube.com/watch?v=sJiw-edttDY
- SciShow. (2016). *Where do domestic cats come from?* YouTube. https://www.youtube.com/watch?v=53Jb7Y6eUUU

Playful adventures situated in the world of nursery rhymes provided multiple opportunities to explore a variety of literacy and art concepts through targeted learning objectives supported by activities, readings, resources, and projects. Partner and small group experiences allow students opportunities to work on a variety of social-emotional skills. Additionally, chapter resources were offered to share with families as a support for the exploration and development of academic, social, and emotional concepts.

First Grade—Fairy Tales

2

Learning experiences should be engaging, joyful, and targeted. Positioning teaching and learning as a classroom community of playful adventures, rather than as a series of academic assignments, is the basis of this chapter. fairy tales offer a foundation for these adventures by providing multiple exposures to child-friendly stories that can be shared at home and school. Additionally, fairy tales offer students opportunities to explore a myriad social and emotional concepts, as well as, literacy learning across content areas.

2.1   Quest Objectives

Learning objectives focused on first grade literacy are based on national and international standards and are provided in a grid format. Objectives explored within the questing systems, can be used as a foundation for future lessons, and/or may be utilized as a review for past learning. A comprehensive overview of the development of quest objectives can be found in the "Getting Started" section of the book. Overarching learning objectives are provided at the beginning of each quest.

To read the grid, look at where the knowledge dimension and cognitive procedural dimension meet (Table 2.1).

2.2   Fairy Tale Four Quest Series Narrative Introduction

Quest #1 focuses on the developing a foundation of understanding through anchor texts, Quest #2 highlights text set resources and the development of speaking and listening skills, Quest #3 targets comprehension through project-based learning,

© The Author(s), under exclusive license to Springer Nature Switzerland AG 2023
J. T. Tussey and L. Haas, *Exploring Genre through Gamified Adventures in Elementary Classrooms*, Springer Texts in Education, https://doi.org/10.1007/978-3-031-41717-7_2

Table 2.1 Learning objective examples for first grade literacy

	Knowledge dimension Factual	Knowledge dimension Conceptual	Knowledge dimension Procedural	Knowledge dimension Metacognitive
Cognitive procedural dimension Remember	Students will be able to list the main events	Students will be able to recognize main characters in the fairy tales	Students will be able to recall the sequence of events	Students will be able to identify and label parts of the story
Cognitive procedural dimension Understand	Students will be able to summarize fairy tales	Students will be able to classify character feelings	Students will be able to clarify the impact of each main event	Students will be able to make predictions about the fairy tales ending
Cognitive procedural dimension Apply	Students will be able to respond to explicit and implicit questions about the fairy tales	Students will be able to provide an overview of the story	Students will be able to carry out tasks related to the story that support deeper understanding	Students will be able to use a variety of art and craft materials to showcase comprehension
Cognitive procedural dimension Analyze	Students will be able to compare and contrast different components of fairy tales	Students will be able to differentiate between the beginning, middle, and end of the fairy tales	Students will be able to integrate problem-solving skills as a way to better explore and comprehend a story	Students will be able to deconstruct the main events of the fairy tales
Cognitive procedural dimension Evaluate	Students will be able to record the progression of their understanding over various fairy tales	Students will be able to determine which fairy tale resource to choose for exploration	Students will be able to judge alternate ways to approach a problem	Students will be able to reflect upon story situations as a means to explore new ways to approach a situation
Cognitive procedural dimension Create	Students will be able to complete projects based on their understanding of the fairy tales	Students will be able to assemble projects based on story to support comprehension	Students will be able to design and discuss alternative story elements associated with fairy tales	Students will be able to create art projects related to and expanded from fairy tales

Concrete ——————————————— > Abstract

2.3 Quest #1—Recall, Summarization, and Writing

and Quest #4 centers on a multimodal art integration. The fairy tales featured throughout the four quest series are the Norwegian fairy tale, *Three Billy Goats Gruff*, the Danish fairy tale, *The Ugly Duckling*, and the English fairy tale, *Jack and the Beanstalk*. An overview of how quests are developed are available in the "Getting Started" section of this book. Additional quest support can be found in the supplemental resource section of this chapter.

Quest Narrative Introduction

Once upon a time, in a land far, far away lived Princess Butterfly and Prince of the Wind. While these two were very different in form, they enjoyed one another's company very much. They first met when the princess was very young and first learning to fly. She was not naturally gifted as a flier and often found herself on the grass rather than perched upon the flowers she so enjoyed. One day, the Prince of the Wind saw the struggling princess and provided a gentle breeze that helped her get from the grass to a beautiful flower. She thanked the prince and asked if he would fly with her again sometime. The prince, having no solid form, was often lonely and was happy to have a new friend. Each day the prince visited, the princesses became more confident and strong in her flying, and the prince became more social and happy. The two were soon inseparable and were happiest when they were together. Every day, as the morning sun began to peak over the horizon, they would set out on a new adventure.

2.3 Quest #1—Recall, Summarization, and Writing

Below, First Grade Quest #1 is presented in a grid format. It was designed to develop student schema through anchor texts as well as support student writing. Differentiated pedagogical strategies are listed in *First Grade Quest #1 Additional Teacher Information* section of the grid provided below.

First grade quest #1 *Fairy tales and wings!*
First grade quest #1 Focus Fairy Tales and Writing
First grade quest #1 overarching objective Develop recall, summarization, and writing skills

(continued)

(continued)

First grade quest #1
Fairy tales and wings!

First grade quest #1 description
Princess Butterfly was just waking up when she heard the leaves begin to rustle in the wind. She knew that meant her dear friend, Prince of the Wind, would soon arrive for their morning adventure. He was such fun!
"Good Morning Princess. I have a surprise for you today."
"Good Morning Prince. I can't wait to hear what you have in store for the day."
"Excellent! Are you ready?"
The princess nodded her head to say that she was ready, and the prince began to move eastward and carried her gently toward a distant body of water. Once they arrived they saw a large duck swimming, and behind her trailed her ducklings
"Oh, Prince, those ducklings are so cute! They all look so much alike, except for the last one in line."
"Yes, that last one is the surprise I wanted to share," said Prince of the Wind
"Why is it so different?" asked Princess Butterfly
"Let's visit Mother Oak, so she can tell you the story of *The Ugly Duckling*," he offered
"I never said the duckling was ugly! I think he's kind of cute. He just looks different from the others," she said in annoyance
"Exactly!" Prince of the Wind agreed as he carried Princess Butterfly to Mother Oak for a story
Once they arrived, Mother Oak agreed to share with the story, but told them they must pay attention to each part of the story in order to truly understand. The prince and princess agreed, so Mother Oak showed the story through a magic portal attached to her truck. Within the portal a string of symbols, https://youtu.be/TyrmcD8Yml0, began to glow

First grade quest #1 assessment and completion
When the story was over, Mother Oak said, "Little ones, this story begins the first quest of today's adventure. Complete this first quest of four and you will be granted access to the next in the series. You must share the story in several ways. First, you must take turns retelling the story to one another so you can recall the sequence of the story and its main events. Next, you will draw and label three main events from the story. Once this is done, share the story and drawing with others, so they may know the story of *The Ugly Duckling*. Once you have shared your knowledge and work, you will earn five XP and gain access to your next quest."

First grade quest #1 additional teacher information
The video students are asked to watch can be found at https://youtu.be/TyrmcD8Yml0 or at https://sn.pub/Kjg4qA . Watching the video can be facilitated either as a whole-group or in small-groups. Teachers may differentiate the summarizing task through student groupings. Additionally, the writing portion of the task can be supported by providing students with word banks and/or sentence stems. During the sharing portion of this activity, it is recommended that teachers invite faculty and/or staff as audience members. Suggestions include administrative assistants, para-educators, principals, and school nurses. Awarding extra XP is encouraged for work exhibiting notable qualities. Examples include, but are not limited to: engagement and attention to details

2.4 Quest #2—Speaking, Listening, and Resource Exploration

Below you will find First Grade Quest #2. This quest is designed for students to work in partners. Each partner will choose a resource treasure box. Individual students will be responsible for reviewing their treasure box and choosing resources to share with their partner. Next, students will play the telephone game in the same way Princess Butterfly and Prince of the Wind were tasked to do so within the quest narrative. Differentiated pedagogical strategies are listed in *First Grade #2 Additional Teacher Information* section of the grid provided below.

First grade quest #2
Treasure trove of information

First grade quest #2 focus
Speaking and Listening

First grade quest #2 overarching objective
Develop speaking and listening skills through the use of group discussions supported by multiple resources

First grade quest #2 description
Mother Oak was pleased with the way the Princess Butterfly and the Prince of the Wind completed their first quest, and sent them along on their second quest
"Travel north to Grandfather Pine. Once there, ask him if you may search for the fairy tale treasure boxes beneath his pine needles. However, I must warn you, Grandfather Pine may require payment before he grants your request," said Mother Oak
The Princess Butterfly and Prince of the Wind thanked Mother Oak for her help and guidance, and they headed north. Once they arrived, they greeted Father Pine and made their request
"If you would like to search for the treasure boxes, you must first promise to play a game with me once they are found," said Grandfather Pine
The prince and princess agreed, so Grandfather Pine continued, "Each treasure box is a great and wonderful prize. One contains fairy tale books and the other provides digital discoveries. Find each treasure box and explore their contents. Next, choose one item from each treasure box to focus all your attention on. Once you have done so, replace the treasure boxes beneath my pine needles and return to play the promised game."
The prince and princess agreed and went on their treasure hunt

First grade quest #2 assessment and completion
Grandfather Pine began, "You will use what you have learned to play a game. It is called the telephone game and requires you to clearly speak and to pay careful attention. First, the Princess Butterfly will whisper to the Prince of the Wind something she learned from her treasure box. He must listen carefully and then whisper to me what she said. I will listen carefully and then tell you both what I heard. The Princess Butterfly will tell us if I understood the message, or if I left something out. When the princess checks my story, this will also help the prince know if he understood the message clearly as well. Next, the Prince of the Wind will start the game. We may repeat the game as many times as we like. You will both earn an additional 15 XP for clearly speaking and carefully listening throughout the game."

(continued)

(continued)

First grade quest #2
Treasure trove of information

First grade quest #2 additional teacher information
Resources for this quest can be found in the section titled *Books: Treasure Box of Fairy Tales* and *Digital Discoveries: Treasure Box of Fairy Tales* within this chapter and at https://sn.pub/Kjg4qA . Teachers may differentiate this task through student groupings based on academic literacy level, native language, and/or social-emotional maturity. Teachers can also differentiate through picture support. Awarding extra XP may be offered for encouragement, engagement, and kindness

Books: treasure box of fairy tales

Fiction
- Hoberman, M. (2012). *Very short fairy tales to read together: Very short fairy tales to read together.* Little, Brown Books for Young Readers

Jack and the Beanstalk
- Braun, E. (2011). *Trust me, Jack's beanstalk stinks!: The story of Jack and the beanstalk as told by the giant.* Picture Window Books
- DK. (2019). *Jack and the beanstalk.* DK Children
- Funk, J. (2017). *It's not Jack and the beanstalk (It's not a fairy tale).* Two Lions
- Galdone, P. (2013). *Jack and the beanstalk.* HMH Books for Young Readers
- Kellogg, S. (1997). *Jack and the beanstalk.* HarperCollins
- Ketteman, H. (2012). *Waynetta and the cornstalk: A Texas fairy tale.* Albert Whitman & Company
- Osborne, M. (2005). *Kate and the beanstalk.* Aladdlin
- Ottolenghi, C. (2001). *Jack and the beanstalk.* Brighter Child
- Teague, M. (2017). *Jack and the beanstalk and the french fries.* Orchard Books

Three Billy Goats Gruff
- Galdone, P. (1981). *The three billy goats gruff.* HMH Books for Young Readers
- Loewen, N. (2018). *Listen, my bridge is SO cool!: The story of the three billy goats gruff as told by the Troll.* Picture Window Books
- Mortimer, R. (2010). *The three billy goats fluff.* Scholastic
- Ottolenghi, C. (2009). *The three billy goats gruff.* Brighter Child
- Palatini, M. (2005). *The three silly billies.* Simon & Schuster Books for Young Readers
- Patchett, A. (2020). *Escape goat.* HarperCollins
- Polacco, P. (2006). *G is for goat.* Puffin Books
- Pinkney, J. (2017). *The three billy goats gruff.* Little, Brown Books for Young Readers
- Pye, K. (2020). *Trip trap trouble: A story about the three billy goats gruff and gratitude.* Headstart Thinking
- Shaskan, S. (2013). *The three triceratops tuff.* Beach Lane Books
- Sims, L. (2015). *Goat in a boat.* Usborne Publishing Ltd

(continued)

2.4 Quest #2—Speaking, Listening, and Resource Exploration

(continued)

Books: treasure box of fairy tales

The Ugly Duckling
- Andersen, H. (1999). *The ugly duckling.* Morrow Junior Books
- Child, C. (2017). *The ugly duckling.* Brighter Child
- Claflin, W. (2011). *The uglified ducky.* August House
- Cronin, D. (2004). *Duck for president.* Atheneum Books for Young Readers
- Linville, R. (2019). *The ugly duckling cries: A story to guess the meaning.* Independently published
- Pilgrim, T. (2015). *Angie, the tundra swan.* FriesenPress
- Shannon, D. (2002). *Duck on a bike.* Blue Sky Press
- Tales, T. (2017). *The ugly duckling.* Tiger Tales

Non-fiction
Jack and the Beanstalk
- Aston, S. (2014). *A seed is sleepy.* Chronicle Books
- Beckstrand, K. (2020). *GROW: How we get food from our garden.* Premio Publishing & Gozo Books, LLC
- Berkes, M. (2013). *What's in a garden?* Dawn Publications
- Ehlert, L. (1990). *Growing vegetable soup.* HMH Books for Young Readers
- Gibbons, G. (1991). *From seed to plant.* Holiday House
- Jordan, H. (2015). *How a seed grows.* HarperCollins
- Mattern, J. (2020). *Growing a beanstalk for Jack (fairy tale science).* Focus Readers
- Sealy, G.A. (2017). *How do plants grow?* DaWit Publishing LLC

Three Billy Goats Gruff
- Bradshaw, A, (2020). *The beginner's guide to raising goats: How to keep a happy herd.* Rockridge Press
- Damerow, G. (1993). *Your goats: A kid's guide to raising and showing.* Storey Publishing, LLC
- Dittmer, L. (2020). *Goats.* Creative Paperbacks
- Hirth, S. (2017). *Happy little goats: Lie life like a kid!* Chronicle Books
- Lauricella, L. (2018). *Angel and her wonderful wheels: A true story of a little goat who walked with wheels.* Walter Foster Jr
- Lauricella, L. (2017). *The goats with many coats.* Walter Foster Jr
- MyIncredible World. (2018). *Goats!: A my incredible world picture book for children.* CreateSpace Independent Publishing Platform
- Smith, R., & Davidson, J. (2015). *Goats for kids.* CreateSpace Independent Publishing Platform
- Smith, S. (2014). *Buttons the famous goat.* XLIBRIS
- Stiefel, C. (2013). *Goats on the family farm.* Enslow Publishing, LLC
- Wolfman, J. (2001). *Life on a goat farm.* Lerner Publications

The Ugly Duckling
- Gish, M. (2020). *Swan.* Creative Paperbacks
- Hughes, M. (2004). *Life cycle of a swan.* Pearson PTR Interactive
- London, J. (2009). *Little swan.* Two Lions
- Randolph, J. (2015). *A family of ducks.* The Rosen Publishing Group, Inc
- Strattin, L. (2019). *Facts about the swan.* Independently published
- Steele, L. (2015). *Duck eggs daily: Raising happy, healthy ducks…naturally.* St. Lynn's Press
- Swinson, K. (2020). *Duck keeping: Beginner's guide to successfully raising and keeping ducks.* Independently published
- Szymanski, J. (2018). *National geographic readers: Ducks.* National Geographic Kids

Digital discoveries: treasure box of fairy tales

Articles/Websites
Jack and the Beanstalk
- Albert, S. (2020). *How to grow beans.* Harvest to Table. https://harvesttotable.com/how_to_grow_green_or_snap_bean/#:~:text=Planting%20and%20Spacing%20Beans&text=Plant%20bush%20beans%203%20to,40%20inches%20(101cm)%20apart
- American Literature. (n.d.). *Jack and the beanstalk.* Retrieved November 12, 2020 from https://americanliterature.com/childrens-stories/jack-and-the-beanstalk

Millay, E. (n.d.). *The bean-stalk.* American Literature. https://americanliterature.com/author/edna-st-vincent-millay/poem/the-bean-stalk
- The Fable Cottage. (2020). *Jack and the beanstalk.* Retrieved November 12, 2020 from https://www.thefablecottage.com/english/jack-and-the-beanstalk
- Peep and the Big Wide World. (2020). *Planting bean seeds.* Retrieved November 12, 2020 from http://www.peepandthebigwideworld.com/en/educators/curriculum/family-child-care-educators/plants/activity/guided-activity/157/planting-bean-seeds/#:~:text=Planting%20in%20Soil,using%20the%20water%20spray%20bottle
- The Science Kiddo. (2018). *Growing beans in a bag.* Retrieved November 12, 2020 from https://www.sciencekiddo.com/bean-seed-in-a-bag/

Three Billy Goats Gruff
- American Literature. (n.d.). *The three billy-goats gruff.* Retrieved November 12, 2020 from https://americanliterature.com/childrens-stories/the-three-billy-goats-gruff
- Iowa PBS. (2020). *The three billy goats gruff*. PBS Learning Media. https://iowa.pbslearningmedia.org/resource/c13341b2-5a09-4dcb-aecf-9cdbe10c4c44/c13341b2-5a09-4dcb-aecf-9cdbe10c4c44/
- The Fable Cottage. (2020). *The three billy goats gruff.* Retrieved November 12, 2020 from https://www.thefablecottage.com/english/three-billy-goats-gruff
- World Stories. (n.d.). *The three billy-goats gruff.* Retrieved November 12, 2020 from https://worldstories.org.uk/reader/the-three-billy-goats-gruff/english/254

The Ugly Duckling
- Anderson, H. (n.d.). *The ugly duckling.* American Literature. https://americanliterature.com/author/hans-christian-andersen/short-story/the-ugly-duckling
- Anderson, H. (2020). *The ugly duckling.* Educational Technology Clearinghouse. https://etc.usf.edu/lit2go/68/fairy-tales-and-other-traditional-stories/5107/the-ugly-duckling/
- Morrisey, J. (2020). *The beginner's guide to raising ducklings: Everything you need to know to get started.* Home in the Finger Lakes. https://homeinthefingerlakes.com/beginners-guide-to-ducklings/

Movies/Videos:
Jack and the Beanstalk
- Asha Loves Science. (2016). *Fun science experiments for kids—growing a bean plant* [Video]. YouTube. https://www.youtube.com/watch?v=TqEh7K9pFs8
- British Council. (2019). *How to grow a bean plant* [Video]. YouTube. https://www.youtube.com/watch?v=QGFUWqSt-sI
- Geethanjali Kids. (2016). *Jack and the beanstalk full story* [Video]. YouTube. https://www.youtube.com/watch?v=Hp9oVeSRVWw
- Tunnicliffe, G. (2010). *Jack and the beanstalk.* Screen Media

Three Billy Goats Gruff
- Brody, R. (Director). (2017). *The three billy goats gruff.* Weston Woods
- Cool School (2014). *Three billy goats gruff & the troll* [Video]. YouTube. https://www.youtube.com/watch?v=kTOkbABj3RU
- Queen, A. (2015). *Three billy goats gruff song* [Video]. YouTube. https://www.youtube.com/watch?v=nSST2cH_fH8&list=PLFTVPyk27YBiAyBneOrhFK7GnAnitTduq&index=52

(continued)

(continued)

Digital discoveries: treasure box of fairy tales
The Ugly Duckling   • Antoro. (Director). (2017). *The ugly duckling story.* Eric Dolphy   • Big Family Homestead. (2015). *Raising ducks.* YouTube. https://www.youtube.com/watch?v=hrK9DUV_-2o   • eHow Pets. (2012). *Protecting swans.* YouTube. https://www.youtube.com/watch?v=dsvdJOTYmuo   • Geethanjali. (2017). *The ugly duckling full story* [Video]. YouTube. https://www.youtube.com/watch?v=TyrmcD8Yml0

2.5 Quest #3—Comprehension, Story Extension, and Problem Solving

Below you will find three options for *First Grade Quest #3.* These quests are designed for students to explore concepts through project-based learning. Each option will be divided into two sections. One section will contain the objective and description to be read before beginning the project. The second section, containing the completion and assessment, is to be read after the project is finished. Differentiated pedagogical strategies are listed in *First Grade Quest #3 Additional Teacher Information* section of all three quests in the grids provided below.

Option I—first grade quest #3 *Go This Way!*	Option II—first grade quest #3 *Here We Grow!*	Option III—first grade quest #3 *Where To Go?*
First grade quest #3 focus Comprehension, Story Extension, and Problem-Solving		
Option I—first grade quest #3 overarching objective Utilize gained knowledge and engage in cooperative, project-based learning and problem solving to develop an alternate route for the *Three Billy Goats Gruff*	**Option II—first grade quest #3 overarching objective** Utilize gained knowledge and engage in cooperative, project-based learning and problem solving to develop an observation and recording plan for the growth of magic beans	**Option III—first grade quest #3 overarching objective** Utilize gained knowledge and engage in cooperative, project-based learning and problem solving to develop an alternate way and/or place for the ugly duckling to hide

(continued)

(continued)

Option I—first grade quest #3 *Go This Way!*	Option II—first grade quest #3 *Here We Grow!*	Option III—first grade quest #3 *Where To Go?*
Option I—first grade quest #3 description The Princess Butterfly said, "The telephone game was so much fun! I wonder where we will find our next quest" Grandfather Pine said, "In order to prepare for your next adventure, you must listen to the story, *Three Billy Goats Gruff*. Once you have discussed the story, fly west and visit Sister Hawthorn. She will guide you through your next adventure" The prince and princess listened to the story and discussed its details as they flew west. Upon their arrival, Sister Hawthorn welcomed them with a kind voice "As adventurers, it is important that you learn how to work cooperatively and problem-solve whenever necessary. Review the tale, *Three Billy Goats Gruff* and discuss what other ways the goats may have tried to reach the other side of the river. Once you have a solution, come back to me to discuss and reflect on your solution. After you have reflected and made any necessary revisions, draw a picture of this alternate path"	**Option II—first grade quest #3 description** The Princess Butterfly said "The telephone game was so much fun! I wonder where we will find our next quest" Grandfather Pine said, "In order to prepare for your next adventure, you must listen to the story, *Jack and the Beanstalk*. Once you have discussed the story, fly west and visit Sister Hawthorn. She will guide you through your next adventure" The prince and princess listened to the story and discussed its details as they flew west. Upon their arrival, Sister Hawthorn welcomed them with a kind voice "As adventurers, it is important that you learn how to work cooperatively and develop plans whenever necessary. Review the tale, *Jack and the Beanstalk* and discuss how you might record the growth of your own magic beans. Once you have a plan in place, come back to me to discuss and reflect on your plan. After you have reflected and made any necessary revisions, plant your beans and draw a picture of all the things you should monitor each day to see what might impact growth"	**Option III—first grade quest #3 description** The Princess Butterfly said "The telephone game was so much fun! I wonder where we will find our next quest" Grandfather Pine said, "In order to prepare for your next adventure, you must review the story, *The Ugly Duckling*. Once you have discussed the story, fly west and visit Sister Hawthorn. She will guide you through your next adventure" The prince and princess listened to the story and discussed its details as they flew west. Upon their arrival, Sister Hawthorn welcomed them with a kind voice "As adventurers, it is important that you learn how to work cooperatively and problem-solve whenever necessary. Review the tale, *The Ugly Duckling* and discuss other places or ways that the ugly duckling could have hidden. Once you have discussed and agreed upon a solution, come back to me to discuss and reflect on your solution. Once you have reflected and made the necessary revisions, draw a picture of this new hiding option"

First grade quest #3 assessment and completion
"You will share your newfound knowledge with friends by venturing to other lands and presenting what you have learned through storytelling. Once you have shared your project and your creative problem-solving with others, you will earn an additional 20 XP and be allowed to move forward to the next adventure," said Sister Hawthorn

(continued)

2.6 Quest #4—Art Integration 25

(continued)

Option I—first grade quest #3	Option II—first grade quest #3	Option III—first grade quest #3
Go This Way!	*Here We Grow!*	*Where To Go?*
First grade quest #3 additional teacher information Teachers may differentiate these tasks through student groupings or time on task. Additionally, material choice can be differentiated based on teacher and student choice. It is recommended that students be allowed to present their projects to other classes of children. For Option I, consider offering materials such as string, clay, or pasta that would allow students to create an alternate path in a tangible way. For Option II, consider discussing and sharing images of plants and measurement tools and discuss what they see in those images that they might need to observe with their beans (sunlight, soil, water, rulers, etc.....). For Option III, consider discussing and sharing images with students of animals who have natural ways to camouflage or hide. Awarding extra XP is encouraged for collaboration, cooperation, and creativity		

2.6 Quest #4—Art Integration

Below you will find First Grade Quest #4. These quests are designed for students to explore literacy concepts through art. Each option will be divided into two sections. One section will contain the objective and description to be read before beginning the project. The second section, containing the completion and assessment, is to be read after the project is finished. Differentiated pedagogical strategies are listed in *First Grade Quest #4 Additional Teacher Information* section of all three quests in the grids provided below.

Option I—first grade quest #4	Option II—first grade quest #4	Option III—first grade quest #4
Do Worry, Be Happy!	*Fairy Giant*	*How Do I Look?*
First grade quest #4 focus Literacy development through art exploration		
Option I—first grade quest #4 overarching objective Engage in critical thinking to consider how physical character traits and expressions might portray feelings	**Option II—first grade quest #4 overarching objective** Engage in critical thinking to consider how physical character traits and expressions might portray personality	**Option III—first grade quest #4 overarching objective** Engage in critical thinking to consider how physical appearance might influence character feelings

(continued)

(continued)

Option I—first grade quest #4 *Do Worry, Be Happy!*	Option II—first grade quest #4 *Fairy Giant*	Option III—first grade quest #4 *How Do I Look?*
Option I—first grade quest #4 description The Princess Butterfly said, "Thank you Sister Hawthorne, we had a lot of fun!" "You are welcome, little princess," Sister Hawthorne smiled. "Now, you must travel south and visit Brother Sycamore for your final quest. In order to prepare, you must review the story, *Three Billy Goats Gruff*," Sister Hawthorn said The prince and princess reviewed the story and discussed its details as they flew south. Upon their arrival, Brother Sycamore welcomed them with a booming voice, and said, "Welcome adventurers! Here, in the south, you will use your creativity to make happiness. Consider how the troll in the story, *Three Billy Goats Gruff* is described. What words or images make you think he might be unhappy? How might you change those words or images to make the troll appear happy? Talk to each other and come up with a plan for each of you to draw a happy troll. Once you have a plan, come back to me to discuss and think about your choices. Finally, draw a picture of a happy troll."	**Option II—first grade quest #4 description** The Princess Butterfly said, "Thank you Sister Hawthorne, we had a lot of fun!" "You are welcome, little princess," Sister Hawthorne smiled. "Now, you must travel south and visit Brother Sycamore for your final quest. In order to prepare, you must review the story, *Jack and the Beanstalk*," Sister Hawthorn said The prince and princess reviewed the story and discussed its details as they flew south. Upon their arrival, Brother Sycamore welcomed them with a booming voice, and said, "Welcome adventurers! Here, in the south, you will use your creativity to turn a giant into a fairy. Consider how the giant in the story, *Jack and the Beanstalk* is described. What words or images make you realize he is a big giant? How might you change those words or images to turn the giant into a fairy? Talk to each other and come up with a plan for each of you to draw the giant as a fairy. Remember, the giant would still act the same. Only the appearance of the giant would change. Once you have a plan, come back to me to discuss and think about your choices. Finally, draw a picture of a giant that is now a fairy."	**Option III—first grade quest #4 description** The Princess Butterfly said, "Thank you Sister Hawthorne, we had a lot of fun!" "You are welcome, little princess," Sister Hawthorne smiled. "Now, you must travel south and visit Brother Sycamore for your final quest. In order to prepare, you must review the story, *The Ugly Duckling*," Sister Hawthorn said The prince and princess reviewed the story and discussed its details as they flew south. Upon their arrival, Brother Sycamore welcomed them with a booming voice, and said, "Welcome adventurers! Here, in the south, you will use your creativity to use clothing to influence feelings. Consider how the ugly duckling in the story, *The Ugly Duckling* is described. What words or images make you think the duckling might feel ugly? How might you change those words or images by using clothing to help the duckling feel better? Talk to each other and come up with a plan for each of you to create an outfit. Once you have a plan, come back to me to discuss and think about your choices. Finally, draw a picture of the duckling in your outfit and tell me how you think your outfit makes the duckling feel."

(continued)

2.7 Supplemental Resources

(continued)

Option I—first grade quest #4	Option II—first grade quest #4	Option III—first grade quest #4
Do Worry, Be Happy!	*Fairy Giant*	*How Do I Look?*

First grade quest #4 assessment and completion
"You will share your newfound knowledge and works of art with the community by displaying it in a place of importance. Once you have shared art, you will earn an additional 25 XP. As this is our final quest, I encourage you to continue thinking creatively as you continue to learn through listening to stories, telling stories, watching stories, and eventually reading stories. Give my regards to Grandmother Oak as you return home. Farewell!" waved Brother Sycamore

First grade quest #4 additional teacher information
Teachers may differentiate these tasks through student groupings or time on task. Additionally, material choice can be differentiated based on teacher and student choice. It is recommended that this art be displayed on a bulletin board either in the classroom or hallway. For Option I, consider sharing and discussing images that convey emotions such as photos of people, animals, and even emojis. For Option II, consider discussing how someone acts may influence how they look and show images of animals and people that seem happy versus those that appear mad. For Option III, consider discussing and sharing images with students of different ways for people to dress, including costumes. If available, consider allowing students to wear costumes for a portion of the day and discuss how wearing a costume impacts their feelings. Awarding extra XP is encouraged for collaboration, cooperation, and creativity

2.7 Supplemental Resources

Supplemental resources available in this section can also be found on https://sn.pub/Kjg4qA. These include:

- Reproducible XP score cards
- Additional teacher resources

Fairy Tale Treasure Boxes for Books and Digital Discoveries can also be found on https://sn.pub/Kjg4qA.

First grade Player name(s)			
Quest #1	Quest #1 XP earned	Quest #1 Extra XP earned	Quest #1 Overall XP:
Quest #2	Quest #2 XP earned:	Quest #2 Extra XP earned:	Quest #2 Overall XP:
Quest #3	Quest #3 XP earned:	Quest #3 Extra XP earned:	Quest #3 Overall XP:
Quest #4	Quest #4 XP earned:	Quest #4 Extra XP earned	Quest #4 Overall XP:
	Quest XP total	Extra XP total	Overall XP total

First grade Player name(s)			
Quest #1	Quest #1 XP earned	Quest #1 Extra XP earned	Quest #1 Overall XP
Quest #2	Quest #2 XP earned	Quest #2 Extra XP earned	Quest #2 Overall XP
Quest #3	Quest #3 XP earned	Quest #3 Extra XP earned	Quest #3 Overall XP
Quest #4	Quest #4 XP earned	Quest #4 Extra XP earned	Quest #4 Overall XP
	Quest XP total	Extra XP total	Overall XP total

Additional Teacher Resources

Speaking and Listening Activities

- Students will dress up as a favorite character and share information about them
- Students will perform a Reader's Theater
- Students will select two fairy tales and share how they are the same and how they are different
- Students will develop a vocabulary list from a selected fairy tale and create definitions
- Students will go on a scavenger hunt to find items in a selected fairy tale

Art Activities

- *Three Billy Goats Gruff* The goats are cold! Students will create cold weather clothing for the goats out of a variety of craft materials
- *Jack and the Beanstalk* Jack lost the egg! Students will use plastic eggs to create a new and fancier golden egg for Jack
- *The Ugly Duckling* A beautiful swan! Students create feathers by using construction paper and glue and use these feathers to create a swan

A classroom community of playful adventures, rather than as a series of academic assignments, was the basis of this chapter. Fairy tales offered a foundation for these adventures by providing multiple exposures to child-friendly stories that can be shared at home and school offering opportunities to explore a myriad social and emotional concepts, as well as, literacy learning across content areas. Partner and small group experiences allow students opportunities to work on a variety of social-emotional skills.

Second Grade—Fables

3

Second Grade learning should be engaging and fun! This chapter offers quests based on classic fables that lead students to and through targeted learning objectives incorporating multiple activities, readings, resources, and projects. Chapter resources offer additional opportunities for exploration and support of academic, social, and emotional concepts.

3.1 Quest Objectives

Learning objectives focused on second grade literacy are based on national and international standards and are provided in a grid format. Objectives explored within the questing systems, can be used as a foundation for future lessons, and/or may be utilized as a review for past learning. A comprehensive overview of the development of quest objectives can be found in the "Getting Started" section of the book. Overarching learning objectives are provided at the beginning of each quest.

To read the grid, look at where the knowledge dimension and cognitive procedural dimension meet (Table 3.1).

© The Author(s), under exclusive license to Springer Nature Switzerland AG 2023
J. T. Tussey and L. Haas, *Exploring Genre through Gamified Adventures in Elementary Classrooms*, Springer Texts in Education, https://doi.org/10.1007/978-3-031-41717-7_3

Table 3.1 Learning objective examples for second grade literacy

	Knowledge dimension	Knowledge dimension	Knowledge dimension	Knowledge dimension
	Factual	Conceptual	Procedural	Metacognitive
Cognitive procedural dimension Remember	Students will be able to list important components from various fables	Students will be able to recognize morals of the fables	Students will be able to recall facts to successfully complete the gameplay	Students will be able to identify important details from the fables
Cognitive procedural dimension Understand	Students will be able to summarize the fables to peers and adults	Students will be able to classify which components of the fables should be included in the gameplay	Students will be able to clarify important information from the resource boxes	Students will be able to make predictions about what will happen next in the fables while having discussions with peers and adults
Cognitive procedural dimension Apply	Students will be able to respond to direct questions about the fables	Students will be able to provide clarification and overviews over the fables to peers and adults	Students will be able to carry out the building of project-based tasks	Students will be able to use various materials to construct tools
Cognitive procedural dimension Analyze	Students will be able to compare and contrast different fables	Students will be able to differentiate the moral of the fables	Students will be able to integrate facts from resources into gameplay	Students will be able to deconstruct steps to complete the development of various products
Cognitive procedural dimension Evaluate	Students will be able to record their understanding in writing and visuals	Students will be able to determine their level of understanding because of gameplay	Students will be able to judge important facts from resources	Students will be able to reflect upon information from print and digital resources
Cognitive procedural dimension Create	Students will be able to complete gameplay tasks	Students will be able to assemble projects connected to specific fables	Students will be able to design tools to support main characters	Students will be able to create products using various materials

Concrete ——————————————————— > Abstract

3.2 Fable Four Quest Series Narrative Introduction

Quest #1 focuses on the developing a foundation of understanding through anchor texts, Quest #2 highlights text set resources and the development of speaking and listening skills, Quest #3 targets comprehension through project-based learning, and Quest #4 centers on a multimodal art integration. The fables featured throughout the four quest series are *The Frog and the Ox*, *The Lion and the Mouse*, and *The Tortoise and the Eagle*. An overview of how quests are developed are available in the "Getting Started" section of this book. Additional quest support can be found in the supplemental resource section of this chapter.

> **Quest Narrative Introduction**
> There once was a mighty wolf who lived in the woods. He was large, quick, and feared by all. The wolf was the Emperor of the Woods and valued obedience above all else. In this same set of woods, a little kitten wandered. She was free spirited, brave, and prone to mischief.

3.3 Quest #1—Storytelling and Presenting

Below, Second Grade Quest #1 is presented in a grid format. It was designed to develop student schema through anchor texts as well as support student writing. Differentiated pedagogical strategies are listed in *Second Grade Quest #1 Additional Teacher Information* section of the grid provided below.

Second grade quest #1   *Let's Hear it for fables!*
Second grade quest #1 focus   Storytelling and presenting
Second grade quest #1 overarching objective   Retell the story with descriptive details and create visual display to support presentation
Second grade quest #1 description   The Emperor Wolf stood next to the river and bent down to take a drink. As he bent down, the water began to glow. At that same exact moment, he felt something fall onto his back. He whirled his head around to see a little kitten with a mischievous smile looking directly into his eyes   "Who are you and what are you doing on my back?" said Wolf   "Sorry, I was hiding in the tree when I saw the river begin to glow. I was so startled that I fell," said Kitten   At the same time, both Wolf and Kitten turned back to the river where they witnessed a story about a frog and an ox   https://www.youtube.com/watch?v=-RPfanWSriQ

32   3 Second Grade—Fables

Second grade quest #1
Let's Hear it for fables!

Second grade quest #1 assessment and completion
When the video is over, the teacher will explain that *The Frog and the Ox* begins the first quest in a set of adventures. Students will complete this first quest of four and be granted access to the next in the series. In order to complete the first quest, students must take turns retelling the story to one another using descriptive details. Next, they will develop visual elements to help clarify thoughts and feelings and support their retelling. Last, they will present their retelling to an audience. Once all three activities are complete, students will earn five XP and gain access to the next quest. Reproducible XP cards are available at the end of this chapter and online

Second grade quest #1 additional teacher information
The video students are asked to watch can be found at https://www.youtube.com/watch?v=-RPf anWSriQ or at https://link.springer.com/book/10.1007/978-3-662-59827-6. Watching the video can be facilitated either as a whole-group or in small-groups. Teachers may differentiate the retelling task through student groupings. Teachers may also encourage students to practice retelling the story to the classroom pet or classroom stuffed animals. During the sharing portion of this activity, it is recommended that students from other classes or grade levels become involved. Awarding extra XP is encouraged for work exhibiting notable qualities. Examples include, but are not limited to: engagement, support of others, and time on task

3.4   Quest #2—Speaking, Listening, and Resource Exploration

Below you will find Second Grade Quest #2. This quest is designed for students to work in partners. Each partner will choose a resource treasure box. Individual students will be responsible for reviewing their treasure box and choosing resources to share with their partner. Next, students will play *Clap or Boo* the same way Wolf and Kitten do within the quest narrative. Differentiated pedagogical strategies are listed in *Second Grade #2 Additional Teacher Information* section of the grid provided below.

Second grade quest #2
Fabled Treasure

Second grade quest #2 focus
Speaking and Listening

Second grade quest #2 overarching objective
Develop speaking and listening skills through gameplay and supported by multiple resources

(continued)

3.4 Quest #2—Speaking, Listening, and Resource Exploration

(continued)

Second grade quest #2
Fabled Treasure

Second grade quest #2 description

After watching the story of The Frog and the Ox, Wolf was careful with his words, because he learned that bragging can be bad. Wolf began, "Kitten, you should not be in the woods, because it can be dangerous for someone as tiny as yourself

"Are you bragging about your size? Remember what happened to the Frog? Listen, I have just as much of a right to be in the woods as you. Plus, I know how to pay attention and listen to my surroundings," snapped Kitten

"I was not bragging; however, it appears that you are," said Wolf

"Well, it's not bragging if it's true," said Kitten

Wolf shook his head and said, "Okay, let's play a little game called *Clap or Boo* to see if you are really a great listener."

"Okay, I'll show you!" Kitten grumbled

Wolf, with a slight grin on his face, began, "When I say something good, you clap, and when I say something bad you say 'boo'. Here's the first statement, 'It's a beautiful day!'"

Kitten clapped

"There is plenty to eat," stated Wolf

Kitten clapped

"Kitten is in danger," Wolf said

Kitten booed

"Kitten needs to run from the hungry Wolf," Wolf hissed

Kitten booed

Then, Kitten's eyes went wide with fear and took off running toward the sunset and out of the woods

Once Kitten was out of hearing range, Wolf laughed and laughed and laughed

As Wolf turned to head further into the woods, she stumbled upon two very interesting boxes. His first thought was about how much fun it would be to share these treasures with friends. He even though Kitten would enjoy them too

Second Grade Quest #2 Assessment and Completion

After the students read the quest narrative and explore the fabled treasures, the teacher will explain that *Clap or Boo* is a game about listening and speaking. Students must pay careful attention in order to win the game. The game may be repeated as many times as the teacher likes. Students can earn 15 XP for clearly speaking and carefully listening throughout the game

Second Grade Quest #2 Additional Teacher Information

Resources for this quest can be found in the section titled *Books: Treasure Box of Fables* and *Digital Discoveries: Treasure Box of Fables* within this chapter and at . Teachers may differentiate this task through student groupings based on academic literacy level, native language, and/or social-emotional maturity.. Awarding extra XP may be offered for engagement, kindness, and sportsmanship

Books: treasure box of fables

Fiction
Fables
- Backstein, K. (1992). *The blind men and the elephant.* Cartwheel
- Cleveland, R. (2012). *The bear, the bat, and the dove: Three stories from Aesop.* August House
- Hoberman, M. (2013). *You read to me, I'll read to you: Very short fables to read together.* Little, Brown Books for Young Readers
- Lobel, A. (1983). *Fables.* HarperCollins
- Lobel. A (1986). *Grasshopper on the road*
- Phidal Publishing. (2017). *The frog and the ox.* Phidal Publishing
- Pinkney, J. (2011). *Lion and the mouse.* Walker & Company
- Santore, C. (2018). *Aesop's fables: The classic edition.* Applesauce Press
- Wormell, C. (2005). *Mice, morals, & monkey business.* Running Press Kids

Morals
- Angebrandt, R. (2019). *Honesty: The best me that I can be.* Rose Angebrandt
- Berenstain, S. (1983). *The Berenstain bears and the truth.* Random House for Young Readers
- Carroll, L. (2019). *It wasn't me!: A short story about honesty.* Independently published
- Cook, J. (2015). *Lying up a storm.* National Center for Youth Issues
- Gordon, M. (2019). *When I am angry.* Independently published
- Levy, A. & Levy, G. (2017). *What should Danny do?* Elon Books
- Levy, A. & Levy, G. (2019). *What should Darla do?* Elon Books
- Lewis, B. (2005). *What do you stand for? For kids: A guide to building character.* Free Spirit Publishing

Non-fiction
Animals
- Bloom, S. (2015). *Elephants: A book for children.* Thames & Hudson
- Clarke, G. (2020). *The fascinating animals book for kids: 500 wilds facts.* Rockridge Press
- Hurt, A. (2016). *National geographic readers: Elephants.* National Geographic Kids
- Marsh, L. (2015). *National geographic readers: Lions.* National Geographic Kids
- Schreiber, A. (2013). *National geographic readers: Monkeys* National Geographic Kids
- Smith, R. (2020). *The big book of wild cats: Fun animal facts for kids.* Rockridge Press
- Spelman, L. (2012). *National geographic animal encyclopedia: 2,500 animals with photos, maps, and more!* National Geographic
- Villaneuva, J. (2019). *100 + amazing pictures and photos in this fantastic elephant photo book.* Independently published

Digital discoveries: treasure box of fables

Articles/websites
- Aesop. (2020). *Aesops fables.* Short kid stories. https://www.shortkidstories.com/story/aesops-fables/
- Glass, S. (2003). *The morals of Aesop's fables.* Together We Teach. http://www.togetherweteach.com/MoreSayings/morals_of_aesop.htm
- Madrid, A. (2018). *New morals for Aesop's fables.* The Daily. https://www.theparisreview.org/blog/2018/11/07/new-morals-for-aesops-fables/
- Stories for Kids. (2020). *What are fables?* Retrieved November 4, 2020 from https://www.studentuk.com/category/fable/
- Study.com. (2020). *Who is Aesop?—biography, fables, & morals.* Retrieved November 4, 2020 from https://study.com/academy/lesson/who-is-aesop-biography-fables-morals.html

(continued)

3.5 Quest #3—Comprehensions, Story Extension, and Problem Solving

(continued)

Digital discoveries: treasure box of fables
Movies/videos
• Geethanjali—Cartoons for Kids. (2015). *Aesop's fables—the tortoise and the eagle* [Film]. YouTube. https://www.youtube.com/watch?v=6phRf2nyF0A
• Jolly Kids English. (2019). *Lion and the mouse story in English* [Film]. YouTube. https://www.youtube.com/watch?v=kSkvkoxJZ_Q
• Pinkfong! Kids' Songs & Stories. (2017). *The peacock and the crane—Aesop's fables* [Film]. YouTube. https://www.youtube.com/watch?v=4ZFZaJurU6c
• Pop'n'Olly. (2019). *The blind men & the elephant* [Film]. YouTube. https://www.youtube.com/watch?v=0qs5cg7fZBc
• Trendz, A. (2018). *Short stories for kids: The frog and the ox.* Prime Video
• T-Series Kids Hut. (2016). *Aesop fables for children* [Film]. YouTube. https://www.youtube.com/watch?v=_mIZy1S9sVI

3.5 Quest #3—Comprehensions, Story Extension, and Problem Solving

Below you will find three options for *Second Grade Quest #3*. These quests are designed for students to explore concepts through project-based learning. Each option will be divided into two sections. One section will contain the objective and description to be read before beginning the project. The second section, containing the completion and assessment, is to be read after the project is finished. Differentiated pedagogical strategies are listed in *Second Grade Quest #3 Additional Teacher Information* section of all three quests in the grids provided below.

Option I—second grade quest #3 *Bigger and better!*	**Option II—second grade quest #3** *Operation freedom!*	**Option III—second grade quest #3** *Land the landing!*
Second grade quest #3 focus Comprehension, Story Extension, and Problem-Solving		
Option I—Second grade quest #3 overarching objective Utilize gained knowledge and engage in cooperative, project-based learning and problem solving to create a way that Frog could make himself look bigger without hurting himself	**Option II—second grade quest #3 overarching objective** Utilize gained knowledge and engage in cooperative, project-based learning and problem solving to create a tool to help free animals if they are trapped	**Option III—second grade quest #3 overarching objective** Utilize gained knowledge and engage in cooperative, project-based learning and problem solving to create a device to help Tortoise land safely on the ground

(continued)

(continued)

Option I—second grade quest #3 *Bigger and better!*	Option II—second grade quest #3 *Operation freedom!*	Option III—second grade quest #3 *Land the landing!*
Option I—second grade quest #3 description Wolf knew he would never see Kitten again. He smiled to himself as he remembered how funny she had looked running out of the woods. So, imagine his surprise when less than 30 min after she had run away, she jumped on his back! Again! This time Wolf's eyes were wide, as he looked at the angry kitten "Why are you here?" asked Wolf "I'm here to show you that I'm not scared of you, and to challenge you!" proclaimed Kitten "What now?" asked Wolf "Let's see who can create a way for Frog to look bigger without hurting himself," offered Kitten "Once I win, will you leave?" asked Wolf "Watch out, you sound a little too confident. You are reminding me of Frog," warned Kitten	**Option II—second grade quest #3 description** Wolf knew he would never see Kitten again. He smiled to himself as he remembered how funny she had looked running out of the woods. So, imagine his surprise when less than 30 min after she had run away, she jumped on his back! Again! This time Wolf's eyes were wide, as he looked at the angry kitten "Why are you here?" asked Wolf "I'm here to show you that I'm not scared of you, and to challenge you!" proclaimed Kitten "What now?" asked Wolf "Let's see who can create a tool to help free animals if they are trapped," offered Kitten "Once I win, will you leave?" asked Wolf "Watch out, your confident ways might get you trapped someday," warned Kitten	**Option III—second grade quest #3 description** Wolf knew he would never see Kitten again. He smiled to himself as he remembered how funny she had looked running out of the woods. So, imagine his surprise when less than 30 min after she had run away, she jumped on his back! Again! This time Wolf's eyes were wide, as he looked at the angry kitten "Why are you here?" asked Wolf "I'm here to show you that I'm not scared of you, and to challenge you!" proclaimed Kitten "What now?" asked Wolf "Let's create a device to help Tortoise land safely on the ground," offered Kitten "Once I win, will you leave?" asked Wolf "Watch out, you might find yourself falling from the sky, if you don't stop being so boastful," warned Kitten

Second grade quest #3 assessment and completion
Students will create projects through trial and error and the use of a variety of materials. They will then share their creations with classmates to earn 20 XP and have access to the next adventure

Second grade quest #3 additional teacher information
Teachers may differentiate these tasks through student groupings or time on task. Additionally, material choice can be differentiated based on teacher and student choice. It is recommended that students be allowed to present their projects to other classes of children. For Option I, consider offering materials such as paper, cloth, and glue as well as images of different types of clothing and paper mache objects. For Option II, consider using craft sticks, paper clips, rubber bands and string to develop a new tool. For Option III, consider using cloth, craft sticks, paper bags, and string. Also consider showing students images of parachutes and hang gliders. Awarding extra XP is encouraged for collaboration, cooperation, and creativity

3.6 Quest #4—Art Integration

Below you will find Second Grade Quest #4. These quests are designed for students to explore literacy concepts through art. Each option will be divided into two sections. One section will contain the objective and description to be read before beginning the project. The second section, containing the completion and assessment, is to be read after the project is finished. Differentiated pedagogical strategies are listed in *Second Grade Quest #4 Additional Teacher Information* section of all three quests in the grids provided below.

Option I—second grade quest #4 *Growing frog!*	Option II—second grade quest #4 *Say cheese!*	Option III—second grade quest #4 *Skyward bound!*
Second grade quest #4 focus Literacy development through art exploration		
Option I—second grade quest #4 overarching objective Engage in critical thinking to consider how visual models of characters support comprehension. Create a growing Frog	**Option II—second grade quest #4 overarching objective** Engage in critical thinking to consider how visual models of characters support comprehension. Create a yearbook picture of Lion and Mouse	**Option III—second grade quest #4 overarching objective** Engage in critical thinking to consider how visual models of the setting support comprehension. Create a picture of the sky that Tortoise could have enjoyed
Option I—second grade quest #4 description "That project was actually kind of fun," proclaimed Wolf "It was supposed to teach you a lesson, but I guess it was fun too," grumped Kitten "Let's call a truce. I won't try to run you off, if you can come up with other fun activities," said Wolf Kitten grinned and said, "This means I can jump on your back whenever I want!" "I didn't say that! I am the Emperor of the Woods, after all," announced Wolf "Let's agree to disagree," said Kitten with a mischievous grin. "Now, I've got some markers and balloons. Let's draw Frog's proud face on the balloon, blow it up, and watch him grow!" said Kitten with an excited voice	**Option II—second grade quest #4 description** "That project was actually kind of fun," proclaimed Wolf "It was supposed to teach you a lesson, but I guess it was fun too," grumped Kitten "Let's call a truce. I won't try to run you off, if you can come up with other fun activities," said Wolf Kitten grinned and said, "This means I can jump on your back whenever I want!" "I didn't say that! I am the Emperor of the Woods, after all," announced Wolf "Let's agree to disagree," said Kitten with a mischievous grin. "Now, I've got some paper and drawing supplies, so let's create a yearbook photo of Lion and Mouse!" said Kitten with an excited voice	**Option III—second grade quest #4 description** "That project was actually kind of fun," proclaimed Wolf "It was supposed to teach you a lesson, but I guess it was fun too," grumped Kitten "Let's call a truce. I won't try to run you off, if you can come up with other fun activities," said Wolf Kitten grinned and said, "This means I can jump on your back whenever I want!" "I didn't say that! I am the Emperor of the Woods, after all," announced Wolf "Let's agree to disagree," said Kitten with a mischievous grin. "Now, I've got some colored paper, drawing and painting supplies, and some glue. Let's create a sky that Tortoise would love to see!" said Kitten with an excited voice

(continued)

(continued)

Option I—second grade quest #4 *Growing frog!*	Option II—second grade quest #4 *Say cheese!*	Option III—second grade quest #4 *Skyward bound!*

Second grade quest #4 assessment and completion
Students will share their art projects with others and earn 25 XP. As this is the final quest, encourage students to continue thinking creatively while listening to stories, telling stories, watching stories, and reading stories

Second grade quest #4 additional teacher information
Teachers may differentiate these tasks through student groupings or time on task. Additionally, material choice can be differentiated based on teacher and student choice. It is recommended that this art be displayed on a bulletin board either in the classroom or hallway. For Option I, consider sharing and discussing images of facial features that convey emotion. For Option II, consider providing yearbooks and/or showing images from yearbooks and discuss the different types of photos. For Option III, consider showing images of the sky in different locations and times of day. Also consider showing images of the sky in all types of weather. Awarding extra XP is encouraged for collaboration, cooperation, and creativity

3.7 Supplemental Resources

Supplemental resources available in this section can also be found on https://sn.pub/Kjg4qA. These include:

- Reproducible XP score cards
- Additional teacher resources

Treasure Boxes for Books and Digital Discoveries can also be found on https://sn.pub/Kjg4qA.

Second grade Player name(s)			
Quest #1	Quest #1 XP earned	Quest #1 Extra XP earned	Quest #1 Overall XP
Quest #2	Quest #2 XP earned	Quest #2 Extra XP Earned	Quest #2 Overall XP
Quest #3	Quest #3 XP earned	Quest #3 Extra XP Earned	Quest #3 Overall XP
Quest #4	Quest #4 XP earned	Quest #4 Extra XP Earned	Quest #4 Overall XP
	Quest XP total	Extra XP total	Overall XP total

3.7 Supplemental Resources

Second grade Player name(s)			
Quest #1	Quest #1 XP earned	Quest #1 Extra XP earned	Quest #1 Overall XP
Quest #2	Quest #2 XP earned	Quest #2 Extra XP earned	Quest #2 Overall XP
Quest #3	Quest #3 XP earned	Quest #3 Extra XP earned	Quest #3 Overall XP
Quest #4	Quest #4 XP earned	Quest #4 Extra XP earned	Quest #4 Overall XP
	Quest XP total	Extra XP total	Overall XP total

Additional Teacher Resources

Speaking and Listening Activities

- Students will create a PowerPoint presentation to show your audience the difference between versions of the same story
- Students will create a commercial over your favorite story to convince your audience why it is best
- Students will create a bingo board with characters, setting, plot, and main events
- Students will create a game (Jeapoary, CandyLand, Twister) over the characters, setting, plot, and main events

Art Activities

- *The Lion and the Mouse:* Design and create a tool that you would use to free your own pets if they got caught
- *The Frog and the Ox*: Design and create a way that the frog could have made himself look bigger rather than popping himself
- *The Tortoise and the Eagle*: Design and create a device that Tortoise could have used to help him as he dropped from the sky

This chapter offered quests based on classic fables that led students to and through targeted learning objectives incorporating multiple activities, readings, resources, and projects. Chapter resources offer additional opportunities for exploration and support of academic, social, and emotional concepts for both home and school. Partner and small group experiences allow students opportunities to work on a variety of social-emotional skills.

Third Grade—Folktales

4

Third grade is a time for engaged and joyful learning! This chapter offers quests based on time honored folktales that lead students to and through targeted learning objectives incorporating multiple activities, readings, resources, and projects across content areas. Chapter resources offer additional opportunities for discovery, exploration, and support of academic, social, and emotional concepts.

4.1 Quest Objectives

Learning objectives focused on third grade literacy are based on national and international standards and are provided in a grid format. Objectives explored within the questing systems, can be used as a foundation for future lessons, and/or may be utilized as a review for past learning. A comprehensive overview of the development of quest objectives can be found in the "Getting Started" section of the book. Overarching learning objectives are provided at the beginning of each quest.

To read the grid, look at where the knowledge dimension and cognitive procedural dimension meet (Table 4.1).

4.2 Four Quest Series Narrative Introduction

Quest #1 focuses on the developing a foundation of understanding through anchor texts, Quest #2 highlights text set resources and the development of speaking and listening skills, Quest #3 targets comprehension through project-based learning, and Quest #4 centers on a multimodal art integration. The Folktales featured

© The Author(s), under exclusive license to Springer Nature Switzerland AG 2023
J. T. Tussey and L. Haas, *Exploring Genre through Gamified Adventures in Elementary Classrooms*, Springer Texts in Education, https://doi.org/10.1007/978-3-031-41717-7_4

Table 4.1 Learning objective examples for third grade literacy

	Knowledge dimension	Knowledge dimension	Knowledge dimension	Knowledge dimension
	Factual	Conceptual	Procedural	Metacognitive
Cognitive procedural dimension Remember	Students will be able to list story elements from the folktales	Students will be able to recognize differences between the various folktales	Students will be able to recall important components from the folktale during discussions	Students will be able to identify key information from the resource boxes
Cognitive procedural dimension Understand	Students will be able to summarize information in written form as well as images	Students will be able to classify important story elements from each of the folktales	Students will be able to clarify questions asked by peers and adults	Students will be able to make predictions about which materials to utilize to build the products
Cognitive procedural dimension Apply	Students will be able to respond to questions from peers and adults connected to folktales	Students will be able to provide descriptions of each folktale	Students will be able to carry out project-based tasks	Students will be able to use various materials to develop resources connected to each folktale
Cognitive procedural dimension Analyze	Students will be able to compare and contrast different components from each folktale	Students will be able to differentiate which materials are the best fit to build the products	Students will be able to integrate new information into their gameplay	Students will be able to deconstruct the process of creating products
Cognitive procedural dimension Evaluate	Students will be able to record the understandings of their classmates	Students will be able to determine the best resources to utilize to complete the tasks	Students will be able to judge the level of understanding based on gameplay results	Students will be able to reflect upon their own connections to the folktale
Cognitive procedural dimension Create	Students will be able to complete project-based activities	Students will be able to assemble project-based activities	Students will be able to design tools to support the main characters	Students will be able to create products using a variety of resources

Concrete——————————————————————— > Abstract

4.3 Quest #1—Storytelling and Presenting 43

throughout the four quest series are, *Little Red Riding Hood*, *The Gingerbread Man*, and *The Little Red Hen*. An overview of how quests are developed are available in the "Getting Started" section of this book. Additional quest support can be found in the supplemental resource section of this chapter.

Quest Narrative Introduction
Once upon a time there lived a little rabbit named Blueberry. His fur was jet black, and his nose was rosebud pink. He loved new sites and smells, and he loved to wander. Blueberry was always on the go, much to his mother's frustration. However, Blueberry felt each road presented a new adventure, and he was eager to try them all.

4.3 Quest #1—Storytelling and Presenting

Below, Third Grade Quest #1 is presented in a grid format. It was designed to develop student schema through anchor texts as well as support student writing. Differentiated pedagogical strategies are listed in *Third Grade Quest #1 Additional Teacher Information* section of the grid provided below.

Third grade quest #1
Folktales Across the Land!

Third grade quest #1 focus
Storytelling and Presenting

Third grade quest #1 overarching objective
Retell the story with descriptive details and create visual display to support presentation

Third grade quest #1 description
Blueberry, the adventurous bunny, decided to take a stroll after a delicious lunch of stewed cabbage and carrots. His mother warned him not to venture too far from home and told him to be back before dark. But, Blueberry didn't pay attention to his mother's warnings and began to wander down a path just past where he usually took his after lunch stroll. Soon, the sun began to set, and Blueberry realized he was in an unfamiliar place. When he turned around to head back home, the single path was suddenly two. One went right, and one went left. As he approached the fork in the road, he noticed a sign. Blueberry approached it carefully, and when he got close, a video began to play
https://www.youtube.com/watch?v=hTrxnTJTTro

Third grade quest #1 assessment and completion
When the video is over, the teacher will explain that *Little Red Riding Hood* begins the first quest in a set of adventures. Students will complete this first quest of four and be granted access to the next in the series. In order to complete the first quest, students must take turns retelling the story to one another using descriptive details. Next, they will develop visual elements to help clarify thoughts and feelings and support their retelling. Last, they will present their retelling to an audience. Once all three activities are complete, students will earn five XP and gain access to the next quest. Reproducible XP cards are available at the end of this chapter and online

44 4 Third Grade—Folktales

Third grade quest #1 additional teacher information
The video students are asked to watch can be found at https://www.youtube.com/watch?v=hTr
xnTJTTro or at https://sn.pub/Kjg4qA. Watching the video can be facilitated either as a
whole-group or in small-groups. Teachers may differentiate the retelling task through student
groupings. Teachers may also encourage students to practice retelling the story to students from
other classes or grade levels. During the sharing portion of this activity, it is recommended that
adults throughout the school become involved. This could include volunteers, office staff,
cafeteria workers, custodians, etc..... Awarding extra XP is encouraged for work exhibiting
notable qualities. Examples include, but are not limited to: engagement, support of others, and
time on task

4.4 Quest #2—Speaking, Listening, and Resource Exploration

Below you will find Third Grade Quest #2. This quest is designed for students to
work in partners. Each partner will choose a resource treasure box. Individual students
will be responsible for reviewing their treasure box and choosing resources
to share with their partner. Next, students will play *Thumbs Up, Thumbs Down* the
same way Blueberry does within the quest narrative. Differentiated pedagogical
strategies are listed in *Third Grade #2 Additional Teacher Information* section of
the grid provided below.

Third grade quest #2
Folklore Treasure

Third grade quest #2 focus
Speaking and Listening

Third grade quest #2 overarching objective
Develop speaking and listening skills through gameplay and supported by multiple resources

Third grade quest #2 description
After watching the story of *Little Red Riding Hood*, Blueberry became very aware there might
be dangers lurking in the woods. This realization made him hesitate in choosing a path. One
path was curved and lined with flowers and the other led directly to a bench down the way.
Blueberry had been so busy daydreaming during his walk that he wasn't sure which one was
the way home. As tears began to well up in his eyes a little caterpillar inched its way across
Blueberry's foot
"Hello," said the caterpillar
"Hello," said a startled Blueberry
"Are you alright?" asked the caterpillar
"I can't remember which path to take to get home," whined Blueberry
"Maybe I can help. Let's play a game. It's called *Thumbs Up, Thumbs Down*. If I say something
that is true about the path home, give me a thumbs up. If I say something that is false, give me a
thumbs down," explained the caterpillar
"It's worth a try," said Blueberry
"Great! The path that brought you here had a sweet smell," said the caterpillar
Blueberry gave a thumbs down
"The path that brought you here was straight, like an arrow," said the caterpillar

4.4 Quest #2—Speaking, Listening, and Resource Exploration

Blueberry gave a thumbs up

"The path that brought you here had sounds like the buzzing of bees," said the caterpillar

Blueberry gave another thumbs down

"The path that brought you here had a place for you to sit and rest," said the caterpillar

Blueberry gave a thumbs up

"Well, I think we just figured out which path brought you here!" exclaimed the caterpillar

"You're right! Thank you so much! I must hurry home now before it is completely dark. Thank you very much!" shouted Blueberry as he began making his way home

"Wait! Make sure you look through the treasure boxes under the bench before you go any further. They will help you, through examples of how to think through your problems," said the caterpillar

Third grade quest #2 assessment and completion

After the students read the quest narrative and explore the folklore treasures, the teacher will explain that *Thumbs Up, Thumbs Down* is a game about listening and speaking. Students must pay careful attention in order to win the game. The game may be repeated as many times as the teacher likes. Students can earn 15 XP for clearly speaking and carefully listening throughout the game

Third grade quest #2 additional teacher information

Resources for this quest can be found in the section titled *Books: Treasure Box of Folktales* and *Digital Discoveries: Treasure Box of Folktales* within this chapter and at https://sn.pub/Kjg4qA. Teachers may differentiate this task through student groupings based on academic literacy level, native language, and/or social-emotional maturity. Awarding extra XP may be offered for engagement, kindness, and sportsmanship

---

Books: treasure box of folktales

Fiction

Little Red Riding Hood

- Daly, N. (2007). *Pretty salma: A little red riding hood story from Africa.* Clarion Books
- Funk, J. (2020). *It's not little red riding hood (It's not a fairy tale).* Two Lions
- Ernst, L. (1998). *Little red riding hood—a newfangled prairie tale*
- Forward, T. (2006). *The wolf's story.* Walker Books Ltd
- Funk, J. (2020). *It's not little red riding hood (It's not a fairy tale).* Two Lions
- Marshall, J. & Perrault, C. (1993). *Red riding hood.* Picture Puffins
- Ransom, C. (2001). *Little red riding hood.* Brighter Child
- Schwartz, C. (2014). *Ninja red riding hood.* G.P. Putnams Sons Books for Young Readers
- Shaskan, T. (2014). *Honestly, red riding hood was rotten!: The story of little red riding hood as told by the wolf.* Picture Window Book
- Smith, A. (2016). *Little red and the very hungry lion.* Scholastic Press
- Urbantoons & Kl'el, K. (2020). *Little red riding hood (African American children's books).* Independently published

Books: treasure box of folktales

The Little Red Hen
- Young, E. (1996). *Lon po po: A red-riding hood story from China.* Puffin Books
- Ada, A. (2004). *With love, little red hen.* Atheneum Books for Young Readers
- Fields, T. (2007). *Burro's tortillas.* Sylvan Dell Publishing
- Forest, H. (2015). *The little red hen: An old fable.* August House
- Galdone, P. (1985). *The little red hen.* Clarion Books
- Granowsky, A. (1995). *Help yourself, little red hen.* Steck-Vaughn
- Helakoski, L. (2008). *Big chickens.* Puffin Books
- Murray, A. (2019). *The little green hen.* Candlewick
- NA. (2011). *The sly fox and the little red hen.* Dreamland Publications
- Ottolenghi, C. (2001). *The little red hen.* Brighter Child
- Simon, F. (2011). *Runaway duckling.* Orion
- Stevens, J. (2011). *The little red pen.* HMH Books for Young Readers
- Sturges, P. (2002). *The little red hen (makes a pizza).* Puffin Books
- Wood, S. (2019). *Holy squawkamole!: Little red hen makes guacamole.* Sterling Children's Book

Gingerbread Man
- Armour, P. (2005). *Stop that pickle.* HMH Books for Young Readers
- Brett, J. (2003). *Gingerbread baby.* G.P. Putman's Sons Books for Young Readers
- Brett, J. (2008). *Gingerbread friends.* G.P. Putman's Sons Books for Young Readers
- Dixon, S. (2018). *The gingerbread man 2: What happened later?* Independently published
- Ernst, L. (2006). *The gingerbread girl.* Dutton Books for Young Readers
- Kimmel, E. (2016). *The runaway tortilla.* WestWinds Press
- Kladstrup, K. (2012). *The gingerbread pirates.* Candlewick
- Leigh, C. (2016). *The ninjabread man.* Orchard Books
- McCafferty, C. (2001). *The gingerbread man.* Brighter Child
- Murray, L. (2016). *The gingerbread man loose at the zoo.* G.P. Putman's Sons Books for Young Readers
- Murray, L. (2011). *The gingerbread man loose in the school.* G.P. Putman's Sons Books for Young Readers
- Shulman, L. (2007). *The matzo ball boy.* Puffin Books
- Squires, J. (2006). *The gingerbread cowboy.* HarperCollins
- Stihler, C. (2010). *The sourdough man: An Alaska folktale.* Sasquatch Books/Paws IV Children's Books
- White, T. (2011). *The Gurabia man: The Armenia version of the gingerbread man.* CreateSpace Independent Publishing Platform
- Yerrill, G. (2018). *The gingerbread man.* Parragon Books

Non-fiction
Little Red Riding Hood
- Atinuke. (2019). *Africa, amazing Africa: Country by country.* Walker Books
- Brandenburg, J. & Brandenburg, J. (2018). *Face-to-face with wolves.* National Geographic Kids
- Marsh, L. (2012). *Wolves.* National Geographic Kids
- Perkins, C. & Woolley, T. (2016). *Living in China.* Simon Spotlight
- Wanner, Z. (2019). *Africa.* Children's Press

4.4 Quest #2—Speaking, Listening, and Resource Exploration

Books: treasure box of folktales

The Little Red Hen
- Caughey, M. (2015). *A kid's guide to keep chickens: Best breeds, creating a home, care and handling, outdoor fun, crafts and treats.* Storey Publishing, LLC
- Crelin, S. (2018). *My chickens lay eggs.* FriesenPress
- Damerow, G. (2012). *The chicken encyclopedia: An illustrated reference.* Storey Publishing
- DiSiena, L. & Eliot, H. (2014). *Chickens don't fly: And other fun facts.* Simon and Schuster
- Dittemore, M. (2019). *Keeping chickens: A kid's guide to everything you need to know about breeds, coops, behavior, eggs, and more!* Sky Pony
- Heller, R. (1999). *Chickens aren't the only ones.* Puffin Books
- Reynolds, S. (2015). *The life cycle of a chicken.* The Rosen Publishing Group, Inc
- Schindel, J. (2015). *Busy chickens.* Knopf Books for Young Readers
- Sexton, C. (2012). *The life cycle of a chicken.* Bellwether Media
- Sommer, C. (2018). *Life of chickens.* Advance Publishing
- Steele, L. (2018). *Let's hatch chicks!: Explore the wonderful world of chickens and eggs.* Young Voyageur
- Thomas, I. (2014). *Herietta's guide to caring for your chickens.* Captson

The Gingerbread Man
- Krebs, L. (2008). *Off we go to Mexico.* Barefoot Books
- Medina, C. (2011). *Make a gingerbread man.* Teacher Created Materials
- McDonnell, G. (2011). *Next stop: Mexico.* Teacher Created Materials
- Mills, T. (2016). *Hey kids! Let's visit London England: Fun, facts, and amazing discoveries for kids.* Life Experiences Publishing
- Mrowczynska, A. (2014). *P is for Poland.* Frances Lincoln Children's Books
- Professor, B. (2017). *There's a lot more than pretty windmills in Poland!* Baby Professor
- Perkins, C. (2016). *Living in...Mexico.* Simon Spotlight
- Roberts, J. & Owens, M. (2018). *A kid's guide to Mexico.* CreateSpace Independent Publishing Platform
- Roman, C. (2016). *If you were me and lived in...Poland: A child's introduction to cultures around the world.* CreateSpace Independent Publishing Platform

Digital discoveries: treasure box of folktales

Articles/Websites
Little Red Riding Hood
- Ducksters. (2020). *Africa geography.* Retrieved November 2, 2020 from https://www.ducksters.com/geography/africa.php
- Ducksters. (2020). *China.* Retrieved November 2, 2020 from https://www.ducksters.com/geography/country/china.php
- Kids Encyclopedia Facts. (2020). *Wolf facts for kids.* Retrieved November 2, 2020 from https://kids.kiddle.co/Wolf
- KidZone Animals. (2020). *Wolves.* Retrieved November 2, 2002 from https://www.kidzone.ws/animal-facts/wolves/index.htm
- Kids-World-Travel-Guide. (2020). *Africa facts.* Retrieved November 2, 2020 from https://www.kids-world-travel-guide.com/africa-facts.html
- National Geographic Kids. (2020). *China.* Retrieved November 2, 2020 from https://kids.nationalgeographic.com/explore/countries/china/

Digital discoveries: treasure box of folktales

The Little Red Hen
- Backyard Chickens. (2020). *Learning center.* Retrieved November 20, 2020 from https://www.backyardchickens.com/articles/categories/learning-center.11/
- Editors of Encyclopaedia Britannica. (2020). *Chicken.* Britannica. https://www.britannica.com/animal/chicken

The Gingerbread Man
- Cooking with Kids. (2020). *Corn tortillas.* Retrieved November 3, 2020 from https://cookingwithkids.org/recipe/corn-tortillas/
- How We Montessori. (n.d.). *How to make: Easy pickles with children.* Retrieved November 3, 2020 from https://www.howwemontessori.com/how-we-montessori/2018/10/making-pickles-with-children.html
- Palanjian, A. (2019). *Easy gingerbread cookies.* Yummy Toddler Food. https://www.yummytoddlerfood.com/recipes/desserts/easy-gingerbread-cookies/

Movies/Videos
Little Red Riding Hood
- Educational videos for students. (2017). *10 fun facts about China for children video* [Video].YouTube. https://www.youtube.com/watch?v=iEueKKpWKAI
- Gigglebox. (2019). *Little red riding hood* [Video]. YouTube. https://www.youtube.com/watch?v=LDMWJCrDVMI
- National Geographic Kids. (2018). *Africa: Destination world.* [Video]. YouTube. https://www.youtube.com/watch?v=PSYHMWmyVfo
- Wilkos, V. (Director). (2017). *Red riding hood.* [Film]. Weston Woods

The Little Red Hen
- GeoBeats Science. (2014). *10 things you didn't know about chickens.* YouTube. https://www.youtube.com/watch?v=r_uthujBqSU
- Hobby Farm Nutt. (2017). *Raising chickens 101.* YouTube. https://www.youtube.com/watch?v=1rDArRNSDBE
- Super Simple TV. (2017). *The little red hen.* YouTube. https://www.youtube.com/watch?v=WYwjuufc19Q
- Trevler, D., Gagne, P., & Ellard, M. (Directors). (2017). *The red hen.* Weston Woods

The Gingerbread Man
Movies/Videos
- Geethanjali—Cartoons for Kids. (2016). *The gingerbread man full story* [Video]. YouTube. https://www.youtube.com/watch?v=b03rVld6Onw
- Gigglebox. (2018). *The gingerbread man* [Video]. YouTube. https://www.youtube.com/watch?v=YoQyyB5xvLk

4.5 Quest #3—Comprehension, Story Extension, and Problem Solving

Below you will find three options for *Third Grade Quest #3*. These quests are designed for students to explore concepts through project-based learning. Each option will be divided into two sections. One section will contain the objective and description to be read before beginning the project. The second section, containing the completion and assessment, is to be read after the project is finished. Differentiated pedagogical strategies are listed in *Third Grade Quest #3 Additional Teacher Information* section of all three quests in the grids provided below.

4.5 Quest #3—Comprehension, Story Extension, and Problem Solving

Option I—third grade quest #3 *Let's go!*	Option II—Third grade quest #3 *River crossing!*	Option III—third grade quest #3 *Baking for buddies!*
Third grade quest #3 focus Comprehension, Story Extension, and Problem-Solving		
Option I—third grade quest #3 overarching objective Utilize gained knowledge and engage in cooperative, project-based learning and problem solving to design and create a method of transportation that would help her escape the wolf	**Option II—third grade quest #3 overarching objective** Utilize gained knowledge and engage in cooperative, project-based learning and problem solving to design and create a way for the Gingerbread man to get across the river	**Option III—third grade quest #3 overarching objective** Utilize gained knowledge and engage in cooperative, project-based learning and problem solving to create a recipe for making the bread that Little Red Hen could share
Option I—third grade quest #3 description Now that Blueberry had gone through the treasure boxes and was on his way home, he was feeling much better. As the sun continued to sink toward the horizon, he felt something hit him on the head. When he looked up a family of squirrels throwing acorns in his direction. "Hey, what are you doing?" questioned Blueberry "We were just trying to get your attention. Please help us. We must get this project done before the sun touches the horizon or we will be in big trouble," said the smallest squirrel "What project?" asked Blueberry "Well, we need help designing and creating a method of transportation to help Little Red Riding Hood escape the wolf!" exclaimed the little squirrel Blueberry knew he might be late getting home, but he had to help Little Red Riding Hood. So, Blueberry stayed to help the squirrels	**Option II—Third grade quest #3 description** Now that Blueberry had gone through the treasure boxes and was on his way home, he was feeling much better. As the sun continued to sink toward the horizon, he felt something hit him on the head. When he looked up a family of squirrels throwing acorns in his direction. "Hey, what are you doing?" questioned Blueberry "We were just trying to get your attention. Please help us. We must get this project done before the sun touches the horizon or we will be in big trouble," said the smallest squirrel "What project?" asked Blueberry "Well, we need help designing and creating a way for The Gingerbread Man to get across the river!" exclaimed the little squirrel Blueberry knew he might be late getting home, but he had to help The Gingerbread Man. So, Blueberry stayed to help the squirrels	**Option III—third grade quest #3 description** Now that Blueberry had gone through the treasure boxes and was on his way home, he was feeling much better. As the sun continued to sink toward the horizon, he felt something hit him on the head. When he looked up a family of squirrels throwing acorns in his direction. "Hey, what are you doing?" questioned Blueberry "We were just trying to get your attention. Please help us. We must get this project done before the sun touches the horizon or we will be in big trouble," said the smallest squirrel "What project?" asked Blueberry "Well, we need help creating a recipe for making bread that The Little Red Hen can share with her friends!" exclaimed the little squirrel Blueberry knew he might be late getting home, but he had to help The Little Red Hen. So, Blueberry stayed to help the squirrels

(continued)

(continued)

Option I—third grade quest #3	Option II—Third grade quest #3	Option III—third grade quest #3
Let's go!	*River crossing!*	*Baking for buddies!*

Third grade quest #3 assessment and completion
Students will create projects through trial and error and the use of a variety of materials. They will then share their creations with classmates to earn 20 XP and have access to the next adventure

Third grade quest #3 additional teacher information
Teachers may differentiate these tasks through student groupings or time on task. Additionally, material choice can be differentiated based on teacher and student choice. It is recommended that students be allowed to present their projects to other classes of children and/or different groupings of adults. For Option I, consider offering materials balloons, foil, paper, paper clips, and glue. Additionally, consider offering images of different types of transportation. For Option II, consider using craft sticks, pasta, rubber bands, and string. Consider also offering images of different types of bridges. For Option III, consider using crayons, paper, markers, and paint. Also consider providing students with recipe books and images of bread recipes. Awarding extra XP is encouraged for collaboration, cooperation, and creativity

4.6   Quest #4—Art Integration

Below you will find Third Grade Quest #4. These quests are designed for students to explore literacy concepts through art. Each option will be divided into two sections. One section will contain the objective and description to be read before beginning the project. The second section, containing the completion and assessment, is to be read after the project is finished. Differentiated pedagogical strategies are listed in *Third Grade Quest #4 Additional Teacher Information* section of all three quests in the grids provided below.

Option I—third grade quest #4	Option II—third grade quest #4	Option III—third grade quest #4
Thank you!	*How are you feeling!*	*Let's be friends!*

Third grade quest #4 focus
Literacy development through art exploration

Option I—third grade quest #4 overarching objective	Option II—third grade quest #4 overarching objective	Option III—third grade quest #4 overarching objective
Engage in critical thinking to consider how to best express gratitude. Create a thank you card for the woodsman	Engage in critical thinking to consider how best to develop friendships. Decorate gingerbread man shapes depicting different types of emotions/feelings	Engage in critical thinking to consider how best to engage with friends. Create friendship puppets for social roleplay

(continued)

4.7 Supplemental Resources

(continued)

Option I—third grade quest #4 *Thank you!*	Option II—third grade quest #4 *How are you feeling!*	Option III—third grade quest #4 *Let's be friends!*
Option I—third grade quest #4 description Now that Blueberry had helped the squirrels, he began running toward his home. Just as he reached the front door and saw his mother's face, the last sliver of the sun dropped beneath the horizon. She smiled at Blueberry and proclaimed, "You made it just in time to join us as we each share what we are grateful for today. We are also going to help our friend, Little Red Riding Hood ame a thank you card for the woodsman." Blueberry loved his adventures, but tonight, he was grateful to be home with family and friends	**Option II—third grade quest #4 description** Now that Blueberry had helped the squirrels, he began running toward his home. Just as he reached the front door and saw his mother's face, the last sliver of the sun dropped beneath the horizon. She smiled at Blueberry and proclaimed, "You made it just in time to join us as we each share how important it is to develop our friendships and honor our emotions. We are going to decorate gingerbread men with the emotions we are feeling this evening." Blueberry loved his adventures, but tonight, he was grateful to be home with family	**Option III—third grade quest #4 description** Now that Blueberry had helped the squirrels, he began running toward his home. Just as he reached the front door and saw his mother's face, the last sliver of the sun dropped beneath the horizon. She smiled at Blueberry and proclaimed, "You made it just in time to join us as we make puppets and put on a play about how to be a good friend." Blueberry loved his adventures, but tonight, he was grateful to be home with family

Third grade quest #4 assessment and completion
Students will share their art projects with others and earn 25 XP. As this is the final quest, encourage students to continue thinking creatively while listening to stories, telling stories, watching stories, and reading stories

Third grade quest #4 additional teacher information
Teachers may differentiate these tasks through student groupings or time on task. Additionally, material choice can be differentiated based on teacher and student choice. It is recommended that this art be displayed on a bulletin board either in the classroom or hallway. For Option I, consider sharing and discussing ways to express gratitude. For Option II, consider providing images of emotions and discuss how students might interact with friends when they are angry, excited, happy, or sad. For Option III, consider role playing different ways friends interact with one another. Awarding extra XP is encouraged for collaboration, cooperation, and creativity

4.7 Supplemental Resources

Supplemental resources available in this section can also be found on https://sn.pub/Kjg4qA. These include:

- Reproducible XP score cards
- Additional teacher resources

Treasure Boxes for Books and Digital Discoveries can also be found on https://sn.pub/Kjg4qA.

Third grade Player name(s)			
Quest #1	Quest #1 XP earned	Quest #1 Extra XP earned	Quest #1 Overall XP
Quest #2	Quest #2 XP earned	Quest #2 Extra XP earned	Quest #2 Overall XP
Quest #3	Quest #3 XP earned	Quest #3 Extra XP earned	Quest #3 Overall XP
Quest #4	Quest #4 XP earned	Quest #4 Extra XP earned	Quest #4 Overall XP
	Quest XP total	Extra XP total	Overall XP total

Third grade Player name(s)			
Quest #1	Quest #1 XP earned	Quest #1 Extra XP earned	Quest #1 Overall XP
Quest #2	Quest #2 XP earned	Quest #2 Extra XP earned	Quest #2 Overall XP
Quest #3	Quest #3 XP earned	Quest #3 Extra XP earned	Quest #3 Overall XP
Quest #4	Quest #4 XP earned	Quest #4 Extra XP earned	Quest #4 Overall XP
	Quest XP total	Extra XP total	Overall XP total

Additional Teacher Resources

Speaking and Listening Activities

- Students will create a PowerPoint presentation to show your audience the difference between versions of the same story
- Students will create a commercial over your favorite story to convince your audience why it is best
- Students will create a bingo board with characters, setting, plot, and main events
- Students will create a game (Jeopardy, Candyland, Twister) over the characters, setting, plot, and main events

4.7 Supplemental Resources

Art Activities

- *Little Red Riding Hood:* Little Red Riding Hood needs to thank the woodsman! Create a thank you for her to give
- *Gingerbread Man:* Gingerbread needs friends! Decorate gingerbread men and women on cookies or construction paper
- *Little Red Hen:* Little Red Hen needs new friends! Create puppets of Little Red Hen and her new friends

This chapter offered quests based on time honored folktales that led students to and through targeted learning objectives incorporating multiple activities, readings, resources, and projects across content areas. Chapter resources offer additional opportunities for discovery, exploration, and support of academic, social, and emotional concepts. Resources are available online for use at home and school. Partner and small group experiences allow students opportunities to work on a variety of social-emotional skills.

Fourth Grade—Legends

5

Fourth Grade academic experiences should provide engaged learning! This chapter offers legendary adventures embedded with targeted learning objectives incorporating multiple activities, readings, resources, and projects. Chapter resources offer additional opportunities for exploration and support of academic, social, and emotional concepts.

5.1 Quest Objectives

Learning objectives focused on fourth grade literacy are based on national and international standards and are provided in a grid format. Objectives explored within the questing systems, can be used as a foundation for future lessons, and/ or may be utilized as a review for past learning. A comprehensive overview of the development of quest objectives can be found in the "Getting Started" section of the book. Overarching learning objectives are provided at the beginning of each quest.

To read the grid, look at where the knowledge dimension and cognitive procedural dimension meet (Table 5.1).

© The Author(s), under exclusive license to Springer Nature Switzerland AG 2023
J. T. Tussey and L. Haas, *Exploring Genre through Gamified Adventures in Elementary Classrooms*, Springer Texts in Education, https://doi.org/10.1007/978-3-031-41717-7_5

Table 5.1 Learning objective examples for fourth grade literacy

	Knowledge dimension	Knowledge dimension	Knowledge dimension	Knowledge dimension
	Factual	Conceptual	Procedural	Metacognitive
Cognitive procedural dimension Remember	Students will be able to list parts of the legends	Students will be able to recognize different character traits	Students will be able to recall key components from the legends	Students will be able to identify main events from the legends
Cognitive procedural dimension Understand	Students will be able to summarize the legends	Students will be able to classify details about each legend	Students will be able to clarify questions about the legend	Students will be able to make predictions about ways to help the main characters
Cognitive procedural dimension Apply	Students will be able to respond to questions from peers about the legends	Students will be able to provide clarification to peers about key events in the legends	Students will be able to carry out activities tied to each legend	Students will be able to use a variety of resources to create a game
Cognitive procedural dimension Analyze	Students will be able to select resources to deepen their understanding	Students will be able to differentiate between their connection to the legends and their peers' connections to the legends	Students will be able to integrate details from the legends into games	Students will be able to deconstruct methods to complete projects tied to each legend
Cognitive procedural dimension Evaluate	Students will be able to check their own understanding and peers' understanding using resources	Students will be able to determine resources and tools to develop products connected to each legend	Students will be able to judge peers' understanding of legends	Students will be able to reflect on questions related to each legend
Cognitive procedural dimension Create	Students will be able to generate ideas to develop games	Students will be able to assemble activities to challenge peers' understanding	Students will be able to design products to support each of the main characters	Students will be able to create products related to each legend

Concrete————————————————————————— > Abstract

5.2 Legend Four Quest Series Narrative Introduction

Quest #1 focuses on the developing a foundation of understanding through anchor texts, Quest #2 highlights text set resources and the development of speaking and listening skills, Quest #3 targets comprehension through project-based learning, and Quest #4 centers on a multimodal art integration. The legends featured throughout the four quest series are Davy Crockett, Johnny Appleseed, and Paul Bunyan. An overview of how quests are developed are available in the "Getting Started" section of this book. Additional quest support can be found in the supplemental resource section of this chapter.

> **Quest Narrative Introduction**
> King Arthur was married to the beautiful Guinevere. Guinevere had a little sister named Gabrielle who was intelligent and compassionate. She was also a wonderful storyteller. Gabrielle, better known as Gabby, wanted more than anything to enter the Hall of Legends like her sister and brother-in-law. However, there was much she needed to learn.

5.3 Quest #1—Paraphrasing and Presenting

Below, Fourth Grade Quest #1 is presented in a grid format. It was designed to develop student schema through anchor texts as well as support student writing. Differentiated pedagogical strategies are listed in *Fourth Grade Quest #1 Additional Teacher Information* section of the grid provided below.

Fourth grade quest #1
Presenting Legends!

Fourth grade quest #1 focus
Paraphrasing and Presenting

Fourth grade quest #1 overarching objective
Paraphrase portions of the story and add visual display to support presentation

Fourth grade quest #1 description
Gabby lived in the Realm of Legends, but was no legend herself. In order to become a legend, she needed to gain access to the Hall of Legends. This process required Gabby to learn about legends and tell their stories in unique and engaging ways. As a storyteller, Gabby was confident, but the only legends she knew were her sister and brother-in-law. So, Gabby began her quest to become a legend with the story of Paul Bunyan
https://www.youtube.com/watch?v=O3rZUOJn5W8

58   5 Fourth Grade—Legends

Fourth grade quest #1 assessment and completion
When the video is over, the teacher will explain that Paul Bunyan begins the first quest in a set
of adventures. Students will complete this first quest of four and be granted access to the next
in the series. In order to complete the first quest, students must take turns retelling the story to
one another. Next, they will develop visual elements to enhance and support their paraphrased
retelling. Last, they will present their retelling to an audience. Once all three activities are
complete, students will earn five XP and gain access to the next quest. Reproducible XP cards
are available at the end of this chapter and online

Fourth grade quest #1 additional teacher information
The video students are asked to watch can be found at https://www.youtube.com/watch?v=O3r
ZUOJn5W8 or at https://sn.pub/Kjg4qA. Watching the video can be facilitated either as a
whole-group or in small-groups. Teachers may differentiate the retelling task through student
groupings based on academic literacy level, native language, and/or social-emotional maturity..
During the sharing portion of this activity, it is recommended that students from other classes or
grade levels become involved. Awarding extra XP is encouraged for work exhibiting notable
qualities. Examples include, but are not limited to: support of others and time on task

5.4   Quest #2—Speaking, Listening, and Resource Exploration

Below you will find Fourth Grade Quest #2. This quest is designed for students to
work in partners. Each partner will choose a resource treasure box. Individual students will be responsible for reviewing their treasure box and choosing resources
to share with their partner. Next, students will play *I Went to the Realm and Saw*
the same way Gabby does so within the quest narrative. Differentiated pedagogical
strategies are listed in *Fourth Grade #2 Additional Teacher Information* section of
the grid provided below.

Fourth grade quest #2
Legendary Treasure

Fourth grade quest #2 focus
Speaking and Listening

Fourth grade quest #2 overarching objective
Develop speaking and listening skills through gameplay and supported by multiple resources

Fourth grade quest #2 description
After watching Paul Bunyan, Gabby felt inspired! So, she gathered the legendary treasure
boxes and began learning more. Once she had new knowledge she wanted to test herself
So, she asked her sister and brother-in-law, Guinevere and Arthur, for help. She asked them to
play the game, *I Went to the Realm and Saw*. This game was a great way for her to practice her
knowledge of legendary creatures and develop her listening skills. Plus it was a lot of fun. To
begin, the three of them stood in a circle and took turns in a counter-clockwise manner. Gabby
went first

5.4 Quest #2—Speaking, Listening, and Resource Exploration

Gabby said, "I went to the realm and saw a unicorn"

Next, Guinevere said, "I went to the realm and saw a unicorn and a minotaur."

Then Arthur said, "I went to the realm and saw a unicorn, a phoenix, and a dragon."

It was Gabby's turn again, and she said, "I went to the realm and saw a unicorn, a phoenix, a dragon, and a griffin."

Guinevere said, "I went to the realm and saw a unicorn, a phoenix, a griffin, and a mermaid."

Gabby and Arthur got very excited and both shouted, "You forgot the dragon!"

All three burst in in giggles and started the game over

Once the game was over, Arthur gifted Gabby with three treasure boxes filled with legends and said, "Thank you for inviting us to play! Now, take this gift of two treasure boxes to support your quest to become a legend."

Fourth grade quest #2 assessment and completion

After the students read the quest narrative and explore the legendary treasures, the teacher will explain that *I Went to the Realm and Saw* is a game about listening and speaking. Students must pay careful attention in order to win the game. The game may be repeated as many times as the teacher likes. Students can earn 15 XP for clearly speaking and carefully listening throughout the game

Fourth grade quest #2 additional teacher information

Resources for this quest can be found in the section titled *Books: Treasure Box of Legends* and *Digital Discoveries: Treasure Box of Legends* within this chapter and at https://sn.pub/Kjg4qA. Teachers may differentiate this task through student groupings based on academic literacy level, native language, and/or social-emotional maturity. Awarding extra XP may be offered for engagement, kindness, and sportsmanship

Books: treasure box of legends

Fiction

Davy Crockett

- Kunstler, J. (1995). *Davy Crockett: The legendary frontiersman.* Simon & Schuster
- Meister, C. (2014). *Davy Crockett and the great Mississippi snag.* Picture Window Books
- Schanzer, R. (2001). *Davy Crockett saves the world.* HarperCollins

Johnny Appleseed

- Braun, E. (2014). *Johnny Appleseed plants trees across the land.* Picture Window Books
- Harrison, D. (2001). *Johnny Appleseed: My story.* Random House Books for Young Readers
- Holub, J. (2015). *Who was Johnny Appleseed?* Penguin Workshop
- Kurtz, J. (2004). *Johnny Appleseed.* Simon Spotlight
- Lindbergh, R. (1993). *Johnny Appleseed.* Little, Brown Books for Young Readers

Paul Bunyan

- Gleeson, B. (2013). *Paul Bunyan.* Rabbit Ears Entertainment
- Harris, D. (2008). *Paul Bunyan: My story.* Random House Books for Young Readers
- Hickey, B. (2020). *Finding Paul Bunyan.* Independently published
- Houran, L. (2020). *The tale of Paul Bunyan.* Golden Books
- Kellogg, S. (2004). *Paul Bunyan.* HarperCollins

Books: treasure box of legends

Other Cultures
- Aardema, V. (2004). *Why mosquitoes buzz in people's ears: A West African tale.* Puffin/Dial
- Cleveland, R. (2006) *The magic apple: A Middle Eastern folktale.* August House
- Cleveland, R. (2012). *Clever monkey: A folktale from West Africa.* August House
- Cleveland, R. (2012). *Clever monkey rides again.* August House
- Cleveland, R. (2006). *How Tiger got his stripes: A folktale from Vietnam.* August House
- DeSpain, P. (2007). *The magic pot.* August House
- Gerson, M. (1995). *Why the sky is far away: A Nigerian folktale.* Little, Brown Books for Young Reader
- Harcourt School Publishers. (2017). *Anansi the spider: A tale from the Ashanti.* Henry Holt and Company
- Hamilton, M. (2006). *A tale of two frogs.* August House
- Norfolk, B. (2012). *Anansi and the tug o' war.* August House

Non-fiction
Davy Crockett
- Adler, D. (1996). *A picture book of Davy Crockett.* Holiday House
- Herman, G. (2013). *Who was Davy Crockett?* Penguin Workshop
- Krensky, S. (2004). *Davy Crockett: A life on the frontier.* Simon Spotlight
- River, C. (2013). *History for kids: The illustrated life of Davy Crockett.* Charles River Editors
- Sullivan, G. (2002). *In their own words: Davy Crockett.* Scholastic Inc

Johnny Appelseed
- Dickmann, N. (2010). *An apple's life.* Heinemann
- Esbaum, J. (2009). *Apples for everyone.* National Geographic Kids
- Faulkner, M. (2005). *A day at the apple orchard.* Scholastic
- Geister-Jones, S. (2020). *At the apple orchard.* Little Blue Readers
- Gibbons, G. (2001). *Apples.* Holiday House

Paul Bunyan
- Brannigan, G. (2015). *Hey! Mr. logger.* CreateSpace Independent Publishing Platform
- Conroy, D. (2015). *Oxen: A teamster's guide to raising, training, driving, & showing.* Storey Publishing, LLC
- Lindsey M. (2020). *Draft animals: 100 answers for harnessing animal power.* Homestead on the Range
- Livingston, M. (2017). *Timber!* Red Tall Publishing
- Livingston, M. (2017). *Timber in the working forest.* Red Tail Publishing

Digital discoveries: treasure box of legends

Davy Crockett
Articles/Websites
- Biography. (2019). *Davy Crockett biography.* Retrieved November 3, 2020 from https://www.biography.com/military-figure/davy-crockett
- History.com Editors. (2019). *Davy Crockett.* History. https://www.history.com/topics/westward-expansion/davy-crockett
- Lofaro, M. (2018). *David "Davy" Crockett.* Tennessee Encyclopedia. https://tennesseeencyclopedia.net/entries/davy-crockett/

5.4 Quest #2—Speaking, Listening, and Resource Exploration

Digital discoveries: treasure box of legends

Johnny Appleseed
Articles/Websites
- Biography. (2020). *Johnny Appleseed.* Retrieved November 2, 2020 from https://www.biography.com/historical-figure/johnny-appleseed
- Boeckmann, C. (2020). *Growing apples: Planting apple trees and harvesting apples.* The Old Farmer's Almanac. https://www.almanac.com/plant/apples
- Editors of Encyclopedia Britannica. (2020). *Was Johnny Appleseed a real person?* Britannica. https://www.britannica.com/story/was-johnny-appleseed-a-real-person
- Extension Utah State University. (2019). *Apples.* Retrieved November 3, 2020 from https://extension.usu.edu/yardandgarden/fruits/apples
- Puchko, K. (2017). *9 facts that tell the true story of Johnny Appleseed.* Mental Floss. https://www.mentalfloss.com/article/62113/9-facts-tell-true-story-johnny-appleseed

Paul Bunyan
Articles/Websites
- Lam, B. (2016). *The life of a lumberjack.* The Atlantic. https://www.theatlantic.com/business/archive/2016/11/logger/507848/
- Living History Farms. (2015). *Training new oxen.* Retrieved November 3, 2020 from https://www.lhf.org/2015/01/training-new-oxen/
- Paul Bunyan Trail. (2020). *Paul Bunyan's Tall Tale.* Retrieved November 3, 2020 from https://www.paulbunyantrail.com/tall-tale/
- The Editors of Encyclopedia Britannica. (2020). *Paul Bunyan.* Britannica. https://www.britannica.com/topic/Paul-Bunyan

Movies/Videos
Davy Crockett
Movies/Videos
- Biography. (2020). *Davy Crockett—remember Davy Crockett.* [Video]. Retrieved November 3, 2020 from https://www.biography.com/video/davy-crockett-remember-davy-crockett-2080047800
- Forster, N. (Director). (1955). *Davy Crockett, king of the wild frontier.* [Film]. Walt Disney Pictures

Johnny Appleseed
Videos/Movies
- Little Cozy Nook. (2019). *Johnny Appleseed READ ALOUD for kids* [Video]. YouTube. https://www.youtube.com/watch?v=P-E4assINhY
- RecipeLion. (2010). *Growing apples: How to grow apple trees.* [Video]. YouTube. https://www.youtube.com/watch?v=GRtOdaMKaII
- The History Guy: History Deserves to be Remembered. (2020). *Johnny Appleseed: Man behind the legend* [Video]. YouTube. https://www.youtube.com/watch?v=MKs0VJbB0R4

Paul Bunyan
Movies/Videos
- Cognocentrics. (2012). *The west coast logging legacy.* [Video]. YouTube. https://www.youtube.com/watch?v=vFoqbU5XKL4
- National Geographic. (2010). *Sustainable logging.* [Video]. YouTube. https://www.youtube.com/watch?v=H-Cn1FwuRpg
- Ross, L. (Director). (2016). *Bunyan & Babe.* [Film]. Cinedigm
- Rural Heritage. (2010) *Training oxen.* [Video]. YouTube. https://www.youtube.com/watch?v=ul2PFDdeJ2k
- The Rusty Grapple. (2018). *Life of the Alaskan logger.* [Video]. YouTube. https://www.youtube.com/watch?v=Ee--KqTCI_s

5.5   Quest #3—Comprehension, Story Extension, and Problem Solving

Below you will find three options for *Fourth Grade Quest #3*. These quests are designed for students to explore concepts through project-based learning. Each option will be divided into two sections. One section will contain the objective and description to be read before beginning the project. The second section, containing the completion and assessment, is to be read after the project is finished. Differentiated pedagogical strategies are listed in *Fourth Grade Quest #3 Additional Teacher Information* section of all three quests in the grids provided below.

Option I—fourth grade quest #3 *Which way do I go?*	Option II—fourth grade quest #3 *Plant support!*	Option III—Fourth grade quest #3 *Lumberjack lunch!*
Fourth grade quest #3 focus Comprehension, story extension, and problem-solving		
Option I—fourth grade quest #3 overarching objective Utilize gained knowledge and engage in cooperative, project-based learning and problem solving to develop a new way for Davy Crockett to travel	**Option II—fourth grade quest #3 overarching objective** Utilize gained knowledge and engage in cooperative, project-based learning and problem solving to create a tool to help Johnny Appleseed plant trees	**Option III—fourth grade quest #3 overarching objective** Utilize gained knowledge and engage in cooperative, project-based learning and problem solving to create a way for Paul Bunyan to feed all the hungry lumberjacks
Option I—fourth grade quest #3 description Gabby had a great time playing with her family! Now, she needed to think a little bit deeper about each legend, if she was ever to become one herself. First, she began thinking about Davy Crockett and wished she could someday meet him. She thought about his story, and knew she could have been a great sidekick. So, she began creating a new scene in his story that included her helping him along the way. She imagined she was the Legendary Transportation Chief, Gabby the Great, sent by the dragons themselves to help Davy Crockett develop a new way to travel	**Option II—fourth grade quest #3 description** Gabby had a great time playing with her family! Now, she needed to think a little bit deeper about each legend, if she was ever to become one herself. First, she began thinking about Johnny Appleseed and wished she could someday meet him. She thought about his story, and knew she could have been a great sidekick. So, she began creating a new scene in his story that included her helping him along the way. She imagined she was the Legendary Maker of Tools, General Gabby, sent by the gnomes themselves to help Johnny Appleseed develop a new way to travel	**Option III—fourth grade quest #3 description** Gabby had a great time playing with her family! Now, she needed to think a little bit deeper about each legend, if she was ever to become one herself. First, she began thinking about Paul Bunyan and wished she could someday meet him. She thought about his story, and knew she could have been a great sidekick. So, she began creating a new scene in his story that included her helping him along the way. She imagined she was the Legendary Chef, Golden Gabby, sent by the Golden Goose herself to help Paul Bunyon figure out how to feed all the hungry lumberjacks

5.6 Quest #4—Art Intregration

Option I—fourth grade quest #3 *Which way do I go?*	Option II—fourth grade quest #3 *Plant support!*	Option III—Fourth grade quest #3 *Lumberjack lunch!*
Fourth grade quest #3 assessment and completion Students will create projects through trial and error and through the use of a variety of materials. They will then share their creations with classmates to earn 20 XP and have access to the next adventure		
Fourth grade quest #3 additional teacher information Teachers may differentiate these tasks through student groupings or time on task. Additionally, material choice can be differentiated based on teacher and student choice. It is recommended that students be allowed to present their projects to other classes of children. For Option I, consider offering materials such as paper, building blocks, clay, and images of different types of transportation. For Option II, consider using glue, craft sticks, rubber bands and string to develop a new tool. For Option III, consider using old menus, recipes, calculators, and calendars to help with meal planning. Awarding extra XP is encouraged for collaboration, cooperation, and creativity		

5.6 Quest #4—Art Intregration

Below you will find Fourth Grade Quest #4. These quests are designed for students to explore literacy concepts through art. Each option will be divided into two sections. One section will contain the objective and description to be read before beginning the project. The second section, containing the completion and assessment, is to be read after the project is finished. Differentiated pedagogical strategies are listed in *Fourth Grade Quest #4 Additional Teacher Information* section of all three quests in the grids provided below.

Option I—fourth grade quest #4 *Hats Off!*	Option II—fourth grade quest #4 *Apple Print!*	Option III—fourth grade quest #4 *Which Way Do I Go?*
Fourth grade quest #4 focus Literacy development through art exploration		
Option I—fourth grade quest #4 overarching objective Engage in critical thinking to consider how the clothing supports character traits. Help Davy Crockett develop a hat better suited for the summer months	**Option II—fourth grade quest #4 overarching objective** Engage in critical thinking to consider how resources within the setting support the story. Help Johnny Appleseed write a letter using only apples and paint	**Option III—fourth grade quest #4 overarching objective** Engage in critical thinking to consider how setting supports the story. Help Paul Bunyan create a map using setting descriptions for the loggers to use

Option I—fourth grade quest #4 *Hats Off!*	Option II—fourth grade quest #4 *Apple Print!*	Option III—fourth grade quest #4 *Which Way Do I Go?*
Option I—fourth grade quest #4 description Gabby had such a great time developing a new way for Davy Crockett to travel, and she wanted the fun to continue. So, she asked Arthur and Guinevere to help her make Davy Crockett a new hat. Since he already had a furry one, Gabby thought it would be nice to make him a hat for the summer. The group experimented with different types and shapes of cloth to create a hat. There was a lot of trial and error to discover the type and shape of cloth that would make the best hat, but the effort was worth the reward	**Option II—fourth grade quest #4 description** Gabby had such a great time developing a new tool for Johnny Appleseed, and she wanted the fun to continue. So, she asked Arthur and Guinevere to help her write a letter using only apples and paint. The group experimented with carving letters into the apples and dipping the letters into the paint to create a stamp. There was a lot of trial and error to discover which carvings created the clearest stamps, but the effort was worth the reward	**Option III—fourth grade quest #4 description** Gabby had such a great time developing a way for Paul Bunyan to feed all the hungry lumberjacks, and she wanted the fun to continue. So, she asked Arthur and Guinevere to help her create a map using the setting descriptions for the loggers to use. There was a lot of trial and error to develop a map with all the described landmarks, but the effort was worth the reward

Fourth grade quest #4 assessment and completion
Students will share their art projects with others and earn 25 XP. As this is the final quest, encourage students to continue thinking creatively while listening to stories, telling stories, watching stories, and reading stories

Fourth grade quest #4 additional teacher information
Teachers may differentiate these tasks through student groupings or time on task. Additionally, material choice can be differentiated based on teacher and student choice. It is recommended that this art be displayed on a bulletin board either in the classroom or hallway. For Option I, consider sharing and discussing images of season specific clothing and clothing materials. Also, consider providing examples of hat styles and shapes. For Option II, consider showing images of stamps and discussing ways in which apples can be carved to create letters. For Option III, consider showing images of rudimentary maps and discussing how the setting is described and illustrated in the story. Awarding extra XP is encouraged for collaboration, cooperation, and creativity

5.7 Supplemental Resources

Supplemental resources available in this section can also be found on https://sn.pub/Kjg4qA. These include:

- Reproducible XP score cards
- Additional teacher resources

5.7 Supplemental Resources

Treasure Boxes for Books and Digital Discoveries can also be found on https://sn.pub/Kjg4qA.

Fourth grade
Player name(s)

Quest #1	Quest #1 XP earned	Quest #1 Extra XP earned	Quest #1 Overall XP
Quest #2	Quest #2 XP earned	Quest #2 Extra XP earned	Quest #2 Overall XP
Quest #3	Quest #3 XP earned	Quest #3 Extra XP earned	Quest #3 Overall XP
Quest #4	Quest #4 XP earned	Quest #4 Extra XP earned	Quest #4 Overall XP
	Quest XP total	Extra XP total	Overall XP total

Fourth grade
Player name(s)

Quest #1	Quest #1 XP earned	Quest #1 Extra XP earned	Quest #1 Overall XP
Quest #2	Quest #2 XP earned	Quest #2 Extra XP earned	Quest #2 Overall XP
Quest #3	Quest #3 XP earned	Quest #3 Extra XP earned	Quest #3 Overall XP
Quest #4	Quest #4 XP earned	Quest #4 Extra XP earned	Quest #4 Overall XP
	Quest XP total	Extra XP total	Overall XP total

Additional Teacher Resources

Speaking and Listening Activities

- Students will create a PowerPoint presentation to show your audience the difference between versions of the same story
- Students will create a commercial over your favorite story to convince your audience why it is best
- Students will create a bingo board with characters, setting, plot, main events
- Students will create a game (Jeopardy, Candyland, Twister) over the characters, setting, plot, and main events

Art Activities

- *Johnny Appleseed*: Johnny needs to write home! Create a postcard using apples into different sizes and paint
- *Davy Crockett*: Davy lost his hat! Create a coonskin hat that Davy would wear
- *Paul Bunyan*: Blue ate the map! Create a map for the loggers to use

This chapter offered legendary quests as a support for targeted learning objectives incorporating multiple activities, readings, resources, and projects. Chapter resources, which can be found within the text and online, offer additional opportunities for exploration and support of academic, social, and emotional concepts. Partner and small group experiences allow students opportunities to work on a variety of social-emotional skills.

Fifth Grade—Myths

6

Fifth grade should be full of joyful learning opportunities! This chapter offers quests based on ancient myths that lead students to and through targeted learning objectives incorporating multiple activities, readings, resources, and projects. Chapter resources offer additional opportunities for exploration and support of academic, social, and emotional concepts.

6.1 Quest Objectives

Learning objectives focused on fifth grade literacy are based on national and international standards and are provided in a grid format. Objectives explored within the questing systems, can be used as a foundation for future lessons, and/or may be utilized as a review for past learning. A comprehensive overview of the development of quest objectives can be found in the "Getting Started" section of the book. Overarching learning objectives are provided at the beginning of each quest.

To read the grid, look at where the knowledge dimension and cognitive procedural dimension meet (Table 6.1).

Table 6.1 Learning objective examples for fifth grade literacy

	Knowledge dimension	Knowledge dimension	Knowledge dimension	Knowledge dimension
	Factual	Conceptual	Procedural	Metacognitive
Cognitive procedural dimension Remember	Students will be able to list basic facts about gods and goddesses	Students will be able to recognize different characteristics of gods and goddesses	Students will be able to recall information from the print and digital resources	Students will be able to identify steps required to create products
Cognitive procedural dimension Understand	Students will be able to summarize information about different gods and goddesses	Students will be able to classify new information to support learning	Students will be able to clarify questions from peers and adults	Students will be able to make predictions about actions that gods and goddesses will complete
Cognitive procedural dimension Apply	Students will be able to respond to direct questions while recalling information	Students will be able to provide written and visual clarification of the gods and goddesses	Students will be able to carry out gameplay tasks connected to the gods and goddesses	Students will be able to use new information to demonstrate a high level of understanding
Cognitive procedural dimension Analyze	Students will be able to compare and contrast key components of the gods and goddesses	Students will be able to differentiate key information versus supporting details from the resource files	Students will be able to integrate new information into gameplay	Students will be able to deconstruct areas of confusion about the gods and goddesses during the discussions
Cognitive procedural dimension Evaluate	Students will be able to record their thoughts about the gods and goddesses	Students will be able to determine important information by reviewing print and digital resources	Students will be able to judge peers' understanding during discussions	Students will be able to reflect upon new information during gameplay
Cognitive procedural dimension Create	Students will be able to complete reviews of information over the gods and goddesses	Students will be able to assemble a collection of products	Students will be able to design various products	Students will be able to create products to support gods and goddesses

Concrete ——————————————————————— > Abstract

6.2 Four Quest Series Narrative Introduction

Quest #1 focuses on the developing a foundation of understanding through anchor texts, Quest #2 highlights text set resources and the development of speaking and listening skills, Quest #3 targets comprehension through project-based learning, and Quest #4 centers on a multimodal art integration. The gods and goddess featured throughout the four quest series are from Greek mythology and are Athena, Poseidon, and Zeus. An overview of how quests are developed are available in the "Getting Started" section of this book. Additional quest support can be found in the supplemental resource section of this chapter.

Quest Narrative Introduction

Long ago in a land that hugged the Aegean Sea, there lived mythological beings that both helped and tormented humans. Some of these beings were considered gods and goddesses. They included the wise warrior goddess, Athena; the god of the sea, Poseidon; and the god of thunder, Zeus. Now, Zeus and Poseidon were brothers and Athena was Zeus' daughter. So, not only was this group of mythological beings mighty, they were also family.

6.3 Quest #1—Storytelling and Presenting

Below, Fifth Grade Quest #1 is presented in a grid format. It was designed to develop student schema through anchor texts as well as support student writing. Differentiated pedagogical strategies are listed in *Fifth Grade Quest #1 Additional Teacher Information* section of the grid provided below.

Fifth grade quest #1
Who Said It Was a Myth?

Fifth grade quest #1 focus
Storytelling and Presenting

Fifth grade quest #1 overarching objective
Retell the story with descriptive details and create visual display to support presentation

Fifth grade quest #1 description
The goddess of dessert, Applepie, wanted to hang out with her friends, but her dad said she had to stay at home. He was so boring, and his dad jokes were the worst! He was Cuisine, the god of food, and was always tricking humans into making some of the strangest concoctions. Sometimes they turned out wonderful, but most of the time they were awful. While Applepie's days were filled with sugary delights, she longed for companionship outside of her family. She wanted to get out and meet other gods, goddesses, and humans. So, she reached out to her sister, Pudding, goddess of chocolate, and asked for her advice. Pudding told her of a wise warrior goddess that had many friends and adventures. Applepie was intrigued, and asked where she could find out more. Pudding handed Applepie a magic mirror that showed Applepie the story of Athena
https://www.youtube.com/watch?v=GfJxfniAJro

(continued)

(continued)

Fifth grade quest #1 assessment and completion
When the video is over, the teacher will explain that Athena begins the first quest in a set of adventures. Students will complete this first quest of four and be granted access to the next in the series. In order to complete the first quest, students must take turns retelling the story to one another using descriptive details. Next, they will develop visual elements to help clarify thoughts and feelings and support their retelling. Last, they will present their retelling to an audience. Once all three activities are complete, students will earn five XP and gain access to the next quest. Reproducible XP cards are available at the end of this chapter and online

Fifth grade quest #1 additional teacher information
The video students are asked to watch can be found at https://www.youtube.com/watch?v=GfJ xfniAJro or at https://sn.pub/Kjg4qA. Watching the video can be facilitated either as a whole-group or in small-groups. Teachers may differentiate the retelling task through student groupings based on academic literacy level, native language, and/or social-emotional maturity. Teachers may also encourage students to practice retelling the story to students from other classes or grade levels. During the sharing portion of this activity, it is recommended that adults throughout the school become involved. This could include volunteers, office staff, cafeteria workers, custodians, etc..... Awarding extra XP is encouraged for work exhibiting notable qualities. Examples include, but are not limited to: engagement, support of others, and time on task

6.4 Quest #2—Speaking, Listening, and Resource Exploration

Below you will find Fifth Grade Quest #2. This quest is designed for students to work in partners. Each partner will choose a resource treasure box. Individual students will be responsible for reviewing their treasure box and choosing resources to share with their partner. Next, students will play *Odd One Out* the same way Applepie does within the quest narrative. Differentiated pedagogical strategies are listed in *Fifth Grade #2 Additional Teacher Information* section of the grid provided below.

Fifth grade quest #2
Mythological Treasure

Fifth grade quest #2 focus
Speaking and Listening

Fifth grade quest #2 overarching objective
Develop speaking and listening skills through gameplay and supported by multiple resources

Fifth grade quest #2 description
After watching the adventures of Athena, Applepie began to think about what adventures she might like to try. She'd always wanted to try creating a savory dish; something like chicken fried steak or corn casserole. While she was dreaming up recipes, her sister, Pudding, asked her to play a game that might help her develop her dish. Applepie agreed
"I will say five words and you have to say which one doesn't belong. Ready? Here we go. The words are apple, orange, car, peach, and banana," said Pudding

6.4 Quest #2—Speaking, Listening, and Resource Exploration

"Car!" exclaimed Applepie

"Good, let's try it again. The words are potatoes, squash, tomatoes, plate, and onions," said Pudding

"Plate! Okay, I get it. Let me try. The words are fork, tamales, tacos, enchiladas, and burritos" said Applepie

"Fork!" exclaimed Pudding, and both goddesses began to giggle

"This is fun, and it's giving me lots of ideas for ingredients," Applepie offered

"You think this game has good ideas, you should check out the treasure boxes Dad has stored in the kitchen! You might not find the right recipe, but you might find the inspiration for one," provided Pudding

"I've never seen them before. Let's go check them out!" proclaimed Applepie

Fifth grade quest #2 assessment and completion

After the students read the quest narrative and explore the mythological treasures, the teacher will explain that *Odd One Out* is a game about listening and speaking. Students must pay careful attention in order to win the game. The game may be repeated as many times as the teacher likes. Students can earn 15 XP for clearly speaking and carefully listening throughout the game

Fifth grade quest #2 additional teacher information

Resources for this quest can be found in the section titled *Books: Treasure Box of Myths* and *Digital Discoveries: Treasure Box of Myths* within this chapter and at https://sn.pub/Kjg4qA. Teachers may differentiate this task through student groupings based on academic literacy level, native language, and/or social-emotional maturity. Awarding extra XP may be offered for engagement, kindness, and sportsmanship

Books: treasure box of myths

Fiction
Greek mythology

- Alexander, H. (2011). *A child's introduction to Greek mythology: The stories of the gods, goddesses, heroes, monsters, and other mythical creatures.* Black Dog & Leventhal
- Briggs, K. (2018). *Gods and heroes: Mythology around the world.* Workman Publishing Company
- Chae, Y. (2020). *Goddess power: A kids' book of Greek and Roman mythology: 10 empowering tales of legendary women.* Rockridge Press
- Dinobibi Publishing. (2019). *Greek mythology: History for kids: A captivating guide to Greek myths of Greek gods, goddesses, heroes, and monsters.* Independently published
- Keith, C. (2017). *Greek mythology for kids: Tales of gods.* Independently published
- Lock, D. (2008). *Greek myths.* DK Readers.
- Napoli, D. (2011). *Treasury of Greek mythology: Class stories of gods, goddesses, heroes & monsters.* National Geographic Kids

Athena

- Gagne, T. (2015). *Athena (Kid's guide to mythology).* Mitchell Lane Publishers, Inc
- Holub, J. (2010). *Athena the brain*
- O'Connor, G. (2010). *Olympians: Athena: Grey-eyed goddess.* First Second
- Professor, B. (2017). *Athena: The goddess with the gray eyes—mythology and folklore.* Baby Professor
- Professor, B. (2017). *Ares vs. Athena: Who won the battle? mythology books for kids.* Aladdin

Books: treasure box of myths

Poseidon
- Gagne, T. (2015). *Poseidon (Kids' guide to mythology)*. Mitchell Lane Publishers, Inc
- Holub, J. & Williams, S. (2012). *Poseidon and the sea of fury*. Aladdin
- Jolley, D. (2008). *Odysseus: Escaping Poseidon's curse*. Graphic Universe
- O'Connor, G. (2013). *Olympians: Poseidon: Earth shaker*. First Second
- Professor, B. (2017). *The big three: Zeus, Poseidon and Hades*. Baby Professor
- Temple, T. (2019). *Poseidon: God of the sea and earthquakes*. Child's World

Zeus:
- Boyer, C. (2019). *Zeus the mighty: The quest for the golden fleas*. Under the Stars
- Foley, R. (2012). *Zeus and the rise of the olympians*. Campfire
- Holub, J & Williams, S. (2012). *Zeus and the thunderbolt of doom*. Aladdin
- Nardo, D. (2015). *Zeus (Kids' guide to mythology)*. Mitchell Lane Publishers, Inc
- O'Connor, G. (2010). *Olympians: Zeus: King of the gods*. First Second
- Professor, B. (2017). *The big three: Zeus, Poseidon and Hades*. Baby Professor
- Temple, T. (2019). *Zeus: Kids of the gods, god of sky and storms*. Child's World

Non-fiction
Greece
- Bordessa, K. (2006). *Tools of the ancient Greeks: A kids' guide to the history & science of life in ancient Greece*. Nomad Press
- Fet, C. (2020). *Ancient Greece for kids through the lives of its philosophers, lawmakers, and heroes*. Independently published
- Osborne, M. & Boyce, N. (2004). *Ancient Greece and the Olympics*. Random House Books for Young Readers
- Pearson, A. (2014). *Ancient Greece: Step into the world of ancient Greece from Greek gods, myths, and festivals to the birth of the Olympics*. DK Children
- Sasek, M. (2009). *This is Greece*. Universe

Greek mythology
- Flynn, S. (2018). *Weird but true know-it-all: Greek mythology*. National Geographic Kids
- Hoena, B. (2014). *National geographic kids everything mythology: Being your quest for facts, photos, and fun fit for gods and goddesses*. National Geographic Kids
- Moraes, T. (2019). *Myth atlas: Maps and monsters, heroes and Gods from the twelve mythological worlds*. Blueprints Editions

---

Digital discoveries: treasure box of myths

Articles/websites
Greece
- Donn, L. (n.d.). *Ancient Greece for kids*. Mr. Donn. https://greece.mrdonn.org/
- Graff, R. (2020). *Greece facts*. Kids-World-Travel-Guide. https://www.kids-world-travel-guide.com/greece-facts.html
- History for Kids. (2020). *Guide to ancient Greece*. Retrieved December 9, 2020 from https://www.historyforkids.net/ancient-greece.html
- National Geographic Kids. (2020). *10 facts about Ancient Greece*. Retrieved December 9, 2020 from https://www.natgeokids.com/za/discover/history/greece/10-facts-about-the-ancient-greeks/
- National Geographic Kids. (2020). *Greece*. Retrieved December 9, 2020 from https://kids.nationalgeographic.com/explore/countries/greece/

6.4 Quest #2—Speaking, Listening, and Resource Exploration

Digital discoveries: treasure box of myths

Greek mythology

- Donn, L. (n.d.). *Ancient Greek myths for kids.* Mr. Donn. https://www.greekmyths4kids.com/
- Greek Gods and Goddesses. (2020). *Greek gods & goddesses.* Retrieved December 9, 2020 from https://greekgodsandgoddesses.net/
- History for Kids. (2020. *Greek gods.* Retrieved December 9, 2020 from https://www.historyfo rkids.net/ancient-greek-gods.html
- Rick Riordan. (n.d.). *Meet the Greek gods.* Retrieved December 9, 2020 from https://rickri ordan.com/extra/meet-the-greek-gods/
- Schwichtenberg, M. (2020). *Greek mythology: gods and goddesses.* https://www.halloween costumes.com/greek-mythology-gods-and-goddesses-.html

Athena

- Ducksters. (2020). *Greek mythology: Athena.* Retrieved December 9, 2020 from https://www. ducksters.com/history/ancient_greece/athena.php
- Editors of Encyclopedia Britannica. (2020). *Athena: Greek mythology.* Britannica. https:// www.britannica.com/topic/Athena-Greek-mythology
- Greek Mythology. (2020). *Athena: Greek goddess of wisdom and war.* Retrieved December 9, 2020 from https://www.greekmythology.com/Olympians/Athena/athena.html

Poseidon

- Ducksters. (2020). *Greek mythology: Poseidon.* Retrieved December 9, 2020 from https:// www.ducksters.com/history/ancient_greece/poseidon.php
- Editors of Encyclopaedia Britannica. (2020). *Poseidon: Greek mythology.* Britannica. https:// www.britannica.com/topic/Poseidon
- Greek Mythology. (2020). *Poseidon: Greek god of the sea.* Retrieved December 9, 2020 from https://www.greekmythology.com/Olympians/Poseidon/poseidon.html

Zeus

- Duckster. (2020). *Ancient Greece: Zeus.* Retrieved December 9, 2020 from https://www.duc ksters.com/history/ancient_greece/zeus.php
- Editors of Encyclopaedia Britannica. (2020). *Zeus: Greek god.* Britannica. https://www.britan nica.com/topic/Zeus
- Greek Mythology. (2020). *Zeus: Greek god of the sky and thunder, king of the gods.* Retrieved December 9, 2020 from https://www.greekmythology.com/Olympians/Zeus/zeus.html

Movies/videos

Greece

- Clarendon Learning. (2019). *Ancient Greece for kids.* YouTube. https://www.youtube.com/ watch?v=RchSJSJAbc0
- IntroBooks Education. (2017). *Greek mythology explained.* YouTube. https://www.youtube. com/watch?v=tFuni1vDuTw
- Junior Jetsetters. (2018). *Facts about Greece for children.* YouTube. https://www.youtube. com/watch?v=8sIQv3-lKog
- Smile and Learn. (2020). *Ancient Greece—5 things you should know.* YouTube. https://www. youtube.com/watch?v=oQmtV_ZKUds

Digital discoveries: treasure box of myths

Greek mythology
- The Touring Teacher. (2018). *What is a myth? Exploring Greek mythology.* YouTube. https://www.youtube.com/watch?v=G99aSAONk3s
- Cirla, A. (2013). *The Greek gods.* YouTube. https://www.youtube.com/watch?v=eJCm8W5RZes
- Geethanjali. (2019). *Athena and Poseidon.* YouTube. https://www.youtube.com/watch?v=z410TiEj9hM
- Geethanjali. (2019). *The story of Medusa—Zeus, Hera, and Little Lo.* YouTube. https://www.youtube.com/watch?v=7RTdNnf6cgY

6.5 Quest #3—Comprehension, Story Extension, and Problem Solving

Below you will find three options for *Fifth Grade Quest #3*. These quests are designed for students to explore concepts through project-based learning. Each option will be divided into two sections. One section will contain the objective and description to be read before beginning the project. The second section, containing the completion and assessment, is to be read after the project is finished. Differentiated pedagogical strategies are listed in *Fifth Grade Quest #3 Additional Teacher Information* section of all three quests in the grids provided below.

Option I—fifth grade quest #3 *Safety First!*	Option II—fifth grade quest #3 *Buoyancy Matters!*	Option III—fifth grade quest #3 *Cool Rider!*
Fifth grade quest #3 focus Comprehension, Story Extension, and Problem-Solving		
Option I—fifth grade quest #3 overarching objective Utilize gained knowledge and engage in cooperative, project-based learning and problem solving to design and create body armor for Athena	**Option II—fifth grade quest #3 overarching objective** Utilize gained knowledge and engage in cooperative, project-based learning and problem solving to design and create a ship that can sail in the roughest seas	**Option III—fifth grade quest #3 overarching objective** Utilize gained knowledge and engage in cooperative, project-based learning and problem solving to design and create a chariot for the god of thunder

(continued)

6.6 Quest #4—Art Integration

(continued)

Option I—fifth grade quest #3 *Safety First!*	Option II—fifth grade quest #3 *Buoyancy Matters!*	Option III—fifth grade quest #3 *Cool Rider!*
Option I—fifth grade quest #3 description Now that Applepie had gone through the treasure boxes, she was definitely feeling inspired. She could feel a recipe bubbling up inside and knew it was just a matter of time before she would be able to create a wonderfully savory dish. This excitement about the creative process prompted her to ask Pudding what she thought would be an appropriate way to show her gratitude to the goddess Athena. Pudding suggested that they work together to design and create body armor as a gift for the warrior goddess	**Option II—fifth grade quest #3 description** Now that Applepie had gone through the treasure boxes, she was definitely feeling inspired. She could feel a recipe bubbling up inside and knew it was just a matter of time before she would be able to create a wonderfully savory dish. This excitement about the creative process prompted her to ask Pudding what she thought would be an appropriate way to show her gratitude to the god Poseidon. Pudding suggested that they work together to design and create a ship that could sail in the roughest seas as a gift for Poseidon	**Option III—fifth grade quest #3 description** Now that Applepie had gone through the treasure boxes, she was definitely feeling inspired. She could feel a recipe bubbling up inside and knew it was just a matter of time before she would be able to create a wonderfully savory dish. This excitement about the creative process prompted her to ask Pudding what she thought would be an appropriate way to show her gratitude to Zeus. Pudding suggested that they work together to design and create a chariot, as a gift to Zeus, so that he could ride across the land

Fifth grade quest #3 assessment and completion
Students will create projects through trial and error and the use of a variety of materials. They will then share their creations with classmates to earn 20 XP and have access to the next adventure

Fifth grade quest #3 additional teacher information
Teachers may differentiate these tasks through student groupings or time on task. Additionally, material choice can be differentiated based on teacher and student choice. It is recommended that students be allowed to present their projects to other classes of children and/or different groupings of adults. For Option I, consider offering materials such as foil, paint, paper bags, paper plates, and glue. Additionally, consider offering images of different types of armor. For Option II, consider using cloth craft sticks, feathers, and string. Consider also offering images of different types of boats and ships. For Option III, consider using glue, pasta, and rubber bands. Awarding extra XP is encouraged for collaboration, cooperation, and creativity

6.6 Quest #4—Art Integration

Below you will find Fifth Grade Quest #4. These quests are designed for students to explore literacy concepts through art. Each option will be divided into two sections. One section will contain the objective and description to be read before beginning the project. The second section, containing the completion and assessment, is to be read after the project is finished. Differentiated pedagogical strategies are listed in *Fifth Grade Quest #4 Additional Teacher Information* section of all three quests in the grids provided below.

Option I—fifth grade quest #4 *Crafty!*	Option II—fifth grade quest #4 *Terrific Trident!*	Option III—fifth grade quest #4 *Thunder Crown!*

Fifth grade quest #4 focus
Literacy development through art exploration

Option I—fifth grade quest #4 overarching objective	Option II—fifth grade quest #4 overarching objective	Option III—fifth grade quest #4 overarching objective
Engage in critical thinking to consider how to best inspire creativity. Create a craft idea book for Athena related to wisdom and warfare	Engage in critical thinking to consider how best to develop a magical tool. Create a new trident for Poseidon	Engage in critical thinking to consider how best to develop a symbol for the god of thunder. Create a crown for Zeus

Option I—fifth grade quest #4 description	Option II—fifth grade quest #4 description	Option III—fifth grade quest #4 description
Now that Applepie had worked with Pudding on a project, she was ready for something new. She wanted more than anything for her savory dish to be creative and original. So, she thought what better way to exercise her creative muscles than through art. She also had a newfound appreciation and admiration for Athena and wanted to help the goddess Athena experience creativity too. Applepie asked Pudding to help her develop a wisdom and warfare craft idea book for Athena as a gift to go along with the body armor they had already created	Now that Applepie had worked with Pudding on a project, she was ready for something new. She wanted more than anything for her savory dish to be creative and original. So, she thought what better way to exercise her creative muscles than through art. She also had a newfound appreciation and admiration for Poseidon and wanted to help the god experience creativity too. Applepie asked Pudding to help her develop the most creative and unique trident ever seen to be given to Poseidon as a gift to go along with the boat they had already created	Now that Applepie had worked with Pudding on a project, she was ready for something new. She wanted more than anything for her savory dish to be creative and original. So, she thought what better way to exercise her creative muscles than through art. She also had a newfound appreciation and admiration for Zeus and wanted to help him experience creativity too. Applepie asked Pudding to help her develop the most creative and unique crown ever seen to be given to Zeus as a gift to go along with the chariot they had already created

Fifth grade quest #4 assessment and completion:
Students will share their art projects with others and earn 25 XP. As this is the final quest, encourage students to continue thinking creatively while listening to stories, telling stories, watching stories, and reading stories

Fifth grade quest #4 additional teacher information:
Teachers may differentiate these tasks through student groupings or time on task. Additionally, material choice can be differentiated based on teacher and student choice. It is recommended that this art be displayed on a bulletin board either in the classroom or hallway. For Option I, consider sharing and discussing craft ideas and offer materials such as crayons, paint, and paper. For Option II, consider providing images of tridents along with materials such as clay, glue, pasta, and straws. For Option III, consider offering images of crowns along with materials such as cotton balls, glitter, paper, and sequins.. Awarding extra XP is encouraged for collaboration, cooperation, and creativity

6.7 Supplemental Resources

Supplemental resources available in this section can also be found on https://sn.pub/Kjg4qA. These include:

- Reproducible XP score cards
- Additional teacher resources

Treasure Boxes for Books and Digital Discoveries can also be found on https://sn.pub/Kjg4qA.

Fifth grade Player name(s)			
Quest #1	Quest #1 XP earned	Quest #1 Extra XP earned	Quest #1 Overall XP
Quest #2	Quest #2 XP earned	Quest #2 Extra XP earned	Quest #2 Overall XP
Quest #3	Quest #3 XP earned	Quest #3 Extra XP earned	Quest #3 Overall XP
Quest #4	Quest #4 XP earned	Quest #4 Extra XP earned	Quest #4 Overall XP
	Quest XP total	Extra XP total	Overall XP total

Fifth grade Player name(s)			
Quest #1	Quest #1 XP earned	Quest #1 Extra XP earned	Quest #1 Overall XP
Quest #2	Quest #2 XP earned	Quest #2 Extra XP earned	Quest #2 Overall XP
Quest #3	Quest #3 XP earned	Quest #3 Extra XP earned	Quest #3 Overall XP
Quest #4	Quest #4 XP earned	Quest #4 Extra XP earned	Quest #4 Overall XP
	Quest XP total	Extra XP total	Overall XP Total

78   6 Fifth Grade—Myths

Additional Teacher Resources

Speaking and Listening Activities

- Students will create a PowerPoint presentation to show your audience the difference between versions of the same story
- Students will create a commercial over your favorite story to convince your audience why it is best
- Students will create a bingo board with characters, setting, plot, and main events
- Students will create a game (Jeopardy, Candy Land, Twister) over the characters, setting, plot, and main events

Art Activities

- *Athena:* Athena lost all of her craft ideas! Create a craft idea book for her
- *Poseidon:* Poseidon's horse broke his trident! Create a new trident for him
- *Zeus:* Zeus destroyed his crown by throwing a lightning bolt! Create a new crown for him

This last chapter offers quests based on ancient myths that offer students a roadmap to and through targeted learning objectives incorporating multiple activities, readings, resources, and projects. Chapter resources, conveniently available within the text and online, offer additional opportunities for exploration and support of academic, social, and emotional concepts. Partner and small group experiences allow students opportunities to work on a variety of social-emotional skills.

Printed in the United States
by Baker & Taylor Publisher Services